DEVELOPING
the
LEADER
WITHIN
YOU 2.0

DEVELOPING

the

LEADER

WITHIN

YOU 2.0

JOHN C.
MAXWELL

HARPERCOLLINS
LEADERSHIP

AN IMPRINT OF HARPERCOLLINS

Published by HarperCollins Leadership, an imprint of HarperCollins.

Published in association with Yates & Yates, www.yates2.com.

Unless otherwise noted, Scripture quotations are taken from New American Standard Bible®. Copyright © 1960, 1962, 1963, 1968, 1971, 1972, 1973, 1975, 1977, 1995 by The Lockman Foundation. Used by permission. (www.Lockman.org)

Scripture quotations marked NIV are from the Holy Bible, New International Version®, NIV®. Copyright © 1973, 1978, 1984, 2011 by Biblica, Inc.® Used by permission of Zondervan. All rights reserved worldwide. www.Zondervan.com. The "NIV" and "New International Version" are trademarks registered in the United States Patent and Trademark Office by Biblica, Inc.®

Scripture quotations marked THE MESSAGE are from *The Message*. Copyright © by Eugene H. Peterson 1993, 1994, 1995, 1996, 2000, 2001, 2002. Used by permission of NavPress. All rights reserved. Represented by Tyndale House Publishers, Inc.

ISBN 978-0-7180-74005 (eBook)
ISBN 978-1-4002-01822 (IE)

Library of Congress Cataloging-in-Publication Data

ISBN 978-0-7180-73992
Names: Maxwell, John C., 1947- author.
Title: Developing the leader within you 2.0 / by John C. Maxwell.
Description: Nashville, Tennessee : HarperCollins, [2018] | Includes
 bibliographical references.
Identifiers: LCCN 2017033337 | ISBN 9780718073992
Subjects: LCSH: Leadership.
Classification: LCC HD57.7 .M394 2018 | DDC 658.4/092--dc23 LC record available
at https://lccn.loc.gov/2017033337

Printed in the United States of America
18 19 20 21 22   LSC   10 9 8 7 6 5 4

This book is dedicated to Mark Cole, the CEO of my companies.
No one has served me better.
No one has helped me more.
He shares my vision with clarity.
He directs my mission with consistency.
He handles my business with integrity.
He loves me!

CONTENTS

Preface to the 2.0 Edition

I can hardly believe it's been twenty-five years since I wrote the original manuscript of *Developing the Leader Within You*. When I first put my four-colored pen to paper, I thought I was writing my *one* leadership book. At age forty-five I had been on quite a leadership journey. When I started my professional career as a minister in rural Indiana in 1969, I didn't think about leadership. I just worked hard. It wasn't until I was at my second church in the early '70s that I realized everything rises and falls on leadership. I started my intentional growth journey at that time and targeted leadership as one of the areas where I wanted to grow. While I was leading that second church in Ohio, I began teaching others leadership. In the early '80s, I took on the leadership of a church in San Diego. It eventually became recognized as one of the ten most influential churches in America. While I was there I wrote *Developing the Leader Within You*. At that time I also started getting many more speaking requests. And I started a company to help me train leaders and distribute training resources. The demands of my schedule and the opportunities to train leaders nationally and internationally prompted me to give up my church in 1995. I've spent my time writing, speaking, and training leaders ever since.

But going back to when I wrote the first edition of this book, as I prepared to write it, I thought a lot about the greatest discovery I had made in leading those three organizations: that leadership can be developed. I had developed the leader within me. And my greatest desire was to share my leadership journey with others and teach what I had learned so that they could develop the leaders within them also.

I thought I had much to share from the first twenty-five years of my leadership life, but when I look back now, I'm struck by how much more I've learned in the twenty-five years since then. That should have been no surprise to me, since I've written many additional books on leadership. But sometimes you don't realize how far you've traveled until you go back and look at where you were. It's like going back to the home you grew up in twenty-five years later: it's a lot smaller than you remembered!

I can't tell you how excited I am to share with you the things I've learned since I first wrote this book. There's so much to tell that I can hardly contain myself—or contain it in just ten chapters.

I have extensively rewritten this entire book. That's why I'm calling it 2.0. It still contains the foundational lessons for becoming a good leader. It's still the first book I recommend that people read to start their leadership development journeys. And it's still the book I recommend that leaders use to mentor others in leadership. But I've taken great pains to give it greater depth, to focus it more specifically on a leader's needs. For example, instead of doing general teaching on integrity and attitude, as I did in the original version, I look more specifically at how those characteristics can make someone a better leader.

In addition, I also removed two chapters that were focused on developing staff (which I cover in depth in other books) and replaced them with two new chapters on topics vital to developing you as a leader: servanthood, the heart of the leader, and personal growth, the expansion of leadership. I look back now and think, *How in the world did I miss those the first time around?*

If you read the original version of the book, you're going to be pleased by all the new material and insights I've included in this new 2.0 edition celebrating the book's twenty-fifth anniversary. I can't imagine offering a better leadership tune-up than this.

If this book is new to you, you're in for a treat, because you're going to receive everything you need to take a significant step in your leadership journey. And if you do everything I suggest in the application section at the end of each chapter, you will be amazed at how much your influence, your effectiveness, and your impact will increase in such a short time.

So let's go. Turn the page, and begin developing the leader within you.

Thank you to:
Charlie Wetzel, my writer
Stephanie Wetzel, who edited the first draft
Carolyn Kokinda, who typed my manuscript notes
Linda Eggers, my executive assistant

ONE

THE DEFINITION OF LEADERSHIP:
INFLUENCE

Everyone talks about it; few understand it. Most people desire to cultivate a high capacity for it; few actually do. I can put my hands on more than fifty definitions and descriptions of it from my personal files. If you google it, you'll get more than 760 million results for it. What am I talking about? *Leadership.*

When I wrote the first edition of this book in 1992, people who wanted to succeed in businesses and other organizations focused their attention on management. Every year another management fad seemed to be in fashion. But few people paid any attention to leadership. It wasn't on most people's radar.

I have earned three degrees: a bachelor's, a master's, and a doctorate. Yet I had not taken a single course in leadership during my studies before the 1993 publication of *Developing the Leader Within You.* Why? Because none of the universities I attended offered a single course on the subject.

Today, however, *leadership* is a buzzword. And schools and universities have embraced it. If you wanted to, you could earn an advanced degree in the subject at more than a hundred accredited universities. All three of the universities I attended now offer courses in leadership.

Why has leadership become so important? Because people are recognizing that becoming a better leader changes lives. Everything rises and falls on leadership. The world becomes a better place when people become better leaders. Developing yourself to become the leader you have the potential to be will change *everything* for you. It will add to your effectiveness, subtract from your weaknesses, divide your workload, and multiply your impact.

WHY MANY PEOPLE DON'T DEVELOP AS LEADERS

More and more people recognize the value of good leadership, yet not very many work to become better leaders. Why is that? Despite the widespread prevalence of leadership books and classes, many people think leadership isn't for them. Maybe it's because they make one of these assumptions:

I'm Not a "Born Leader," so I Can't Lead

Leaders are not born. Well, okay, they're *born*. I've never met an unborn leader. (And I wouldn't want to.) What I really mean is that your ability to lead is not set at birth. While it's true that some people are born with more natural gifts that will help them lead at a higher level, everyone has the potential to become a leader. And leadership can be developed and improved by anyone willing to put in the effort.

A Title and Seniority Will Automatically Make Me a Leader

I believe this kind of thinking was more common in my generation and that of my parents, but it can still be seen today. People think they need to be appointed to a positon of leadership, when the reality is that becoming a good leader requires desire and some basic tools. You can have a title and seniority and be incapable of leading. And you can have no title or seniority and be a good leader.

Work Experience Will Automatically Make Me a Leader

Leadership is like maturity. It doesn't automatically come with age. Sometimes age comes alone. Tenure does not create leadership ability. In fact, it's more likely to engender entitlement than leadership ability.

I'm Waiting Until I Get a Position to Start Developing as a Leader

This last assumption has been the most frustrating to me as a teacher of leadership. When I first started hosting leadership conferences, people would say, "If I ever become a leader"—meaning if they were ever appointed to a leadership position—"then maybe I'll come to one of your seminars." What's the problem? As legendary UCLA basketball coach John Wooden said, "When opportunity comes, it's too late to prepare." If you start learning about leadership now, not only will you increase your opportunities, but you'll also make the most of them when they arrive.

HOW WILL YOU DEVELOP THE LEADER WITHIN YOU?

The bottom line is that if you've never done anything to develop yourself as a leader, you can start today. And if you have already begun your leadership journey, you can become a better leader than you already are by intentionally developing the leader within you.

What will that take? That's the subject of this book. These ten chapters contain what I consider to be the ten *essentials* for developing yourself as a leader. I've also created free bonus materials that you can access at MaxwellLeader.com. Included is an assessment that will help you gauge your current leadership ability. I encourage you to take it before reading any further.

Let's start with the most important concept of the ten: *influence*. After more than five decades of observing leaders around the world and many years of developing my own leadership potential, I have come to this conclusion: *Leadership is influence.* That's it—nothing more, nothing less. That's why my favorite leadership proverb is "He who thinketh he leadeth and hath no one following him is only taking a walk." For you to be a leader, someone has to be following you. I love what James C. Georges, founder and chairman of the PAR Group, said in an interview I read years ago: "What is leadership? Remove for a moment the moral issues behind it, and there is only one definition: *Leadership is the ability to obtain followers.*"[1]

> Leadership is the ability
> to obtain followers.
>
> —JAMES C. GEORGES

Anyone—for good or ill—who gets others to follow is a leader. That means Hitler was a leader. (Did you know that *Time* named Hitler their Man of the Year in 1938 because he had greater influence on the world than anyone else?) Osama bin Laden was a leader. Jesus of Nazareth was a leader. So was Joan of Arc. Abraham Lincoln, Winston Churchill, Martin Luther King Jr., and John F. Kennedy were leaders. While the value systems, abilities, and goals of all these people were vastly different, each of them attracted followers. They all had influence.

Influence is the beginning of true leadership. If you mistakenly define leadership as the ability to achieve a position instead of the ability to attract followers, then you will go after position, rank, or title to try to become a leader. But this type of thinking results in two common problems. First, what do you do if you attain the status of a leadership position but experience the frustration of having no one follow you? Second, what if you never achieve the "proper" title? Will you keep waiting to try to make a positive impact on the world?

My goal with this book is to help you understand how influence works, and use it as the starting point for learning how to lead more effectively. Each chapter is designed to help you acquire skills and abilities that further develop you as a leader. With the addition of each skill set, you will become a better leader.

INSIGHTS ABOUT INFLUENCE

Before we get into the particulars of how influence with others works and how to develop it, let's nail down a few important insights about influence:

1. Everyone Influences Someone

My friend Tim Elmore, the founder of Growing Leaders, once told me that sociologists estimate that even the most introverted individual will influence ten thousand other people during his or her lifetime. Isn't that amazing? Every day you influence others. And you are influenced *by* others. That means no one is excluded from being both a leader and a follower.

In any given situation with any group of people, the dynamic of influence is always in play. Let me illustrate. Let's say a child is getting ready for school. During that process, his mother is usually the dominant influence. She may choose what he will eat and what he will wear. When he arrives at school, he may become the influencer in his group of friends. When class begins, his teacher becomes the dominant influencer. After school, when the boy goes out and plays, the neighborhood bully may have the most influence. And at dinnertime, Mom or Dad has the most influence at the table as they eat.

If you are observant, you can discover the prominent leader of any group. Titles and positions don't matter. Just watch the people as they gather. As they work to resolve an issue or make a decision, whose opinion seems most valuable? Who is the person others watch the most when the issue is being discussed? Who is the one with whom people quickly agree? Whom do others defer to and follow? Answers to these questions point you to who the real leader is in a particular group.

You have influence in this world, but *realizing your potential* as a leader is your responsibility. If you put effort into developing yourself as a leader, you have the potential to influence more people and to do so in more significant ways.

2. We Don't Always Know Who or How Much We Influence

One of the most effective ways to understand the power of influence is to think about the times you have been touched in your life by a person or an event. Significant events leave marks on all our lives and memories. For example, ask people born before 1930 what they were doing on December 7, 1941, when they heard that Pearl Harbor was bombed, and they will describe in detail their feelings and surroundings when they heard the terrible news. Ask someone born before 1955 to describe what he or she was doing on November 22, 1963, when the news that John F. Kennedy had been shot was broadcast. Again, you will hear no loss for words. Each generation remembers events that mark them: the day the space shuttle *Challenger* blew up. The tragedy of 9/11. The list goes on. What major event stands out to you? How is that event continuing to influence your thinking and actions?

Now think about the people who influenced you in a powerful way, or the little things that meant a lot to you. I can point to the influence of a camp I attended as a youth and how it helped determine my career choice. My seventh-grade teacher, Glen Leatherwood, began to stir a sense of calling in my life that I continue to live out today in my seventies. When my mother bought bubble lights for our family Christmas tree, there was no way for her to know that they would evoke the feeling of Christmas in me every year. The affirming note I received from a professor in college kept me going at a time when I was doubting myself. My list is endless. So is yours.

We are influenced every day by so many people. Sometimes small things make big impressions. We have been molded into the people we are by those influences. And we mold others, often when we least expect it. Author and educator J. R. Miller said it well: "There have been meetings of only a moment which have left impressions for life, for eternity. No one of us can understand that mysterious thing we call influence . . . yet out of every one of us continually virtue goes, either to heal, to bless, to leave marks of beauty; or to wound, to hurt, to poison, to stain other lives."[2]

3. The Best Investment in Tomorrow Is to Develop Your Influence Today

What's your greatest investment possibility for the future? The stock market? Real estate holdings? More education? All of these things have value. But I would argue that one of the best investments you can make in yourself is to develop your influence. Why? Because if you have the desire to accomplish something, you will be in a better place to do it if others are willing to help.

In the book *Leaders*, Warren G. Bennis and Burt Nanus say, "The truth is that leadership opportunities are plentiful and within reach of most people."[3] That's true in businesses, volunteer organizations, and social groups. If you're an entrepreneur, those opportunities are multiplied exponentially. The question is, will you be ready for them when they come? To make the most of them, you must prepare for leadership today and learn how to cultivate influence and use it positively to make a difference.

Robert Dilenschneider, founder and principal of the Dilenschneider Group and former CEO of the PR firm Hill and Knowlton Strategies, has been one of the nation's major influence brokers for many years. In his book *Power and Influence*, he shares the idea of the "power triangle" to help leaders become more effective. The three components of this triangle are *communication*, *recognition*, and *influence*. Dilenschneider says, "If you are communicating effectively, you will get positive recognition for your communication from the audiences you are trying to influence, which means people will think what you are doing is right and that you are doing it in the right way. When you get positive recognition, your influence grows. You are perceived as competent, effective, worthy of respect—*powerful*. Power comes from remembering and using the linkage of communication, recognition, and influence."[4]

As a young leader, I followed that pathway to better leadership because communication is one of my gifts. As I became a better communicator, I did receive recognition. Soon I was being asked to teach on the subject of leadership. But I also sensed that leadership was more complex than just communication, recognition, and influence. I began thinking about how I could develop a model that would help others understand how influence works, and more importantly, how to develop influence in their own lives. I knew that if the people I helped invested in their influence, they would be able to make a positive impact in their world, wherever that happened to be.

THE FIVE LEVELS OF LEADERSHIP

I began studying influence more carefully, and I also drew upon my own leadership experience and what I observed in leaders I respected and admired. What I discovered is that influence can be developed in five stages. I turned those stages into a tool that I call the 5 Levels of

Leadership. It provides a model of influence that can help you better understand the dynamics of leadership, and it also creates a road map you can follow to develop influence with others. I've been teaching this model of leadership for more than thirty years, and I can't count the number of people it's helped. I hope it helps you in the same way it has others.

The 5 Levels of Leadership

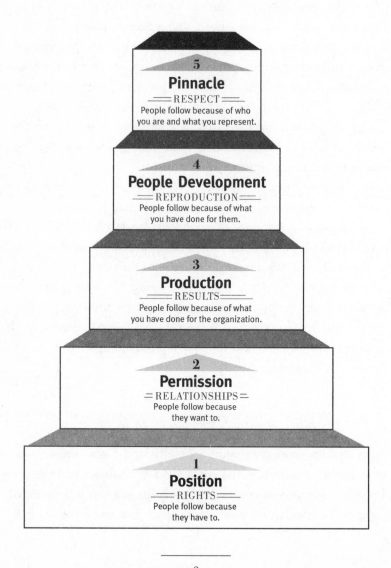

5
Pinnacle
RESPECT
People follow because of who
you are and what you represent.

4
People Development
REPRODUCTION
People follow because of what
you have done for them.

3
Production
RESULTS
People follow because of what
you have done for the organization.

2
Permission
RELATIONSHIPS
People follow because
they want to.

1
Position
RIGHTS
People follow because
they have to.

Let's examine each of the levels. You'll quickly get a handle on how they work.

LEVEL 1: POSITION

The most basic entry level of leadership is the Position level. Why is this the lowest level? Because Position represents leadership *before* a leader has developed any real influence with the people being led. In generations past, people would follow leaders simply because they possessed a title or position of authority. But that is not very common today in American culture. People will follow a positional leader only as far as they *have* to.

When I took my first job as a leader in 1969, people were respectful of me. They were kind. But I had no real influence. I was twenty-two. They could see how little I knew, even if I couldn't. I found out how little influence I had when I led my first board meeting. I started the meeting with my agenda in hand. But then Claude started to talk. He was just an old farmer, but everyone in the room looked to him for leadership. Whatever he said held the most weight. Claude wasn't pushy or disrespectful. He didn't do a power play. He didn't have to. He already had all the power. He just wanted to get things done.

It's very clear to me now that in that first job, I was a leader living on Level 1. All I had going for me at first was my position—along with a good work ethic and a desire to make a difference. I learned more on Level 1 than at any other time in my early years of leading. I figured out pretty quickly that a title and position won't get a person very far in leadership.

People who have been appointed to a position may have authority, but that authority doesn't exceed their job description. Positional leaders have certain *rights*. They have the right to enforce the rules. They have the right to tell people to do their jobs. They have the right to use whatever power they have been granted.

But real leadership is more than having granted authority. Real leadership is being a person others will gladly and confidently follow. Real leaders know the difference between position and influence.

It's the difference between being a boss and being a leader:

Bosses drive workers; leaders coach them.
Bosses depend on authority; leaders depend on goodwill.
Bosses inspire fear; leaders inspire enthusiasm.
Bosses say, "I"; leaders say, "We."
Bosses fix the blame for any breakdown; leaders fix the breakdown.
Bosses know how it is done; leaders show how.
Bosses say, "Go"; leaders say, "Let's go!"

Position is a good place to start in leadership, but it's a terrible place to stay. Anyone who never leads beyond Position depends on territorial rights, protocol, tradition, and organizational charts. These things are not inherently negative—unless they become the basis for authority. They are poor substitutes for leadership skills.

> Position is a good place to start in leadership, but it's a terrible place to stay.

If you've been in a leadership position for any length of time, how do you know whether you are relying too much on your position to lead? Here are three common characteristics of positional leaders:

Positional Leaders Look for Security Based on Title More Than Talent

There's a story about a private during World War I who saw a light in his trench on the battlefield and shouted, "Put out that match!" Much to his chagrin, he discovered that the offender was General "Black Jack" Pershing. Fearing severe punishment, the private tried to stammer out an apology, but General Pershing patted him on the back and said, "That's all right, son. Just be glad I'm not a second lieutenant."

The higher people's level of ability and the resulting influence, the more secure and confident they become. A new second lieutenant might be tempted to rely on his rank and use it as a weapon. A general doesn't need to.

Positional Leaders Rely on Their Leader's Influence Instead of Their Own

Baseball Hall of Famer Leo Durocher, who managed the Giants from 1948 to 1955, was once coaching at first base in an exhibition game played at the United States Military Academy at West Point. During the game, a noisy cadet kept shouting at Durocher, trying to get under his skin.

"Hey, Durocher," he hollered. "How did a little squirt like you get into the major leagues?"

Durocher shouted back, "My congressman appointed me!"[5]

Just because people may be appointed to a position of authority doesn't automatically mean they can develop influence. Because some positional leaders can't and possess no influence or authority of their own, they rely on the authority of their boss or the person who appointed them. Anytime they fear that their team members won't follow them, they're quick to say, "We need to do this because the boss says so." That kind of borrowed authority can wear thin after a while.

Positional Leaders Can't Get People to Follow Them Beyond Their Defined Authority

A common reaction of followers to positional leaders is to do only what's required and nothing more. If you've observed leaders asking people to do something extra, stay late, or go out of their way, only to have the people refuse or say, "That's not my job," then you might be seeing the results of positional leadership. People who define their leadership by position will find themselves in a place where people will do only what's required based on the *rights* granted by that position. People do not become committed to vision or causes led by positional leaders.

If any of these three characteristics describe you, then you may be relying too much on your position, which means you need to work harder at cultivating influence. Until you do, the team you lead will have low energy and you will feel as if every task is a major ordeal. To change that, you'll need to start focusing on the next level of leadership.

LEVEL 2: PERMISSION

My friend and mentor Fred Smith says, "Leadership is getting people to work for you when they are not obligated."[6] That is the essence of the second level of leadership, Permission.

Leaders who remain on the Position level and never develop their influence often lead by intimidation. They are like the chickens that Norwegian psychologist Thorleif Schjelderup-Ebbe studied in developing the "pecking order" principle that is commonly used to describe all kinds of groups. Schjelderup-Ebbe found that in any flock, one hen usually dominates all the others. This dominant hen can peck any other without being pecked in return. The second in the order can peck all the others except the top hen. The rest are arranged in a descending hierarchy, finally ending with one hapless hen who can be pecked by all, but who can peck no one else.

In contrast, Permission is characterized by good *relationships*. The motto on this level could be written as "People don't care how much you know until they know how much you care." True influence begins with the heart, not the head. It flourishes through personal connections, not rules and regulations. The agenda on this level is not pecking order; it's people connection. Leaders who succeed on this level focus their time and energy on the needs and desires of the individuals on their team. And they connect with them.

The classic illustration of someone who didn't do this is Henry Ford in the early days of the Ford Motor Company. He wanted his laborers to work like machines, and he attempted to control their interactions outside of work with rules and regulations. And his focus was totally on his product, the Model T, which he believed was the perfect car, and which he never wanted to change. When people started asking for it in colors other than black, he famously responded, "You can have any color you want as long as it's black."

People who are unwilling or unable to build solid, lasting relationships soon discover that they are also unable to sustain lasting, effective leadership. Needless to say, you can care about people without leading them, but you cannot lead people well without caring about them. People won't go along with you if they cannot get along with you. That's just the way it is.

On Level 2, as you connect with people, build relationships with them, and earn their trust, you begin to develop real influence with them. That makes you want to work together more. It makes you more cooperative with one another. It makes the environment more positive. It boosts everyone's energy. And in work settings, people stay longer and work harder.

> People who are unwilling or unable to build solid, lasting relationships soon discover that they are also unable to sustain lasting, effective leadership.

If you've been given a leadership position, then you've been given your boss's permission to lead. If you've earned influence on Level 2, then you have acquired your people's permission to lead. That's powerful. However, I do have to caution you. Staying too long on this level without adding Level 3 will cause highly motivated people to become restless. So let's talk about Production.

LEVEL 3: PRODUCTION

Nearly anyone can succeed on the first two levels of leadership. People can receive a *position* and develop *permission* with little or no innate leadership ability. It's a fact that if you care about people and are willing to learn how to work with them, you can start to gain influence. But that influence will only go so far. To really get things going, you need to win the Production level.

On Level 3, people get things done. And they help the members of their team get things done. Together they produce *results*. That's when good things really begin to happen for the organization. Productivity goes up. People reach goals. Profit increases. Morale becomes high. Turnover becomes low. Team loyalty increases.

Organizations with leaders who are effective in leading on the first three levels of leadership become highly successful. They start winning. And when they do, they start to benefit from what I call "the Big Mo"— momentum. They grow. They solve problems more easily. Winning becomes normal. Leading becomes easier. Following becomes more fun. The work environment becomes high-energy.

Be aware that most people naturally gravitate to either the Permission or the Production level of leadership, based on whether they tend to be *relationship* people or *results* people. If people naturally build relationships, they may enjoy getting together, but they do it with the sole objective of being together and enjoying one another. If you've ever worked in an environment where meetings are pleasant and everyone gets along—but nothing gets accomplished—then you may have worked with someone who gets Level 2 but not Level 3. (And if you've worked where meetings are productive but relationally miserable, you may have worked with someone who gets Level 3 but not Level 2!) However, as a leader, if you can add *results* to *relationships* and develop a team of people who like each other and get things done, you have created a powerful combination.

Organizations all over the world are searching for people who can produce results, because they understand the impact they can make. One of my all-time favorite stories is about a newly hired traveling salesman named Gooch and the reaction he got from his company's leaders when he sent his first sales report to the home office. It stunned the head of the sales department. Gooch wrote, "I seen this outfit which they ain't never bot a dim's worth of nothin from us and I sole them some goods. I'm now goin to Chicawgo."

Before the man could be given the heave-ho by the sales manager, along came this message from Chicago: "I cume hear and sole them haff a million."

Fearful if he did—and afraid if he didn't—fire the ignorant salesman, the sales manager dumped the problem in the president's lap.

The following morning, the ivory-towered sales department members were amazed to see posted on the bulletin board above the two letters written by the ignorant salesman this memo from the president:

We ben spendin two much time trying to spel instead of trying to sel. Let's watch those sails. I want everybody should read these letters from

Gooch who is on the rode doin a grate job for us and you should go out and do like he done.

I love that story so much I've had it laminated, and I carry it along with a few other "essentials" when I speak. Okay, so if we lead sales-people, we would obviously prefer ones who can both sell and spell. But you get the point. Results speak loudly—to those we work for and to those we lead.

When you lead a productive team of people who like working together, you give others a reason to want to work with you, to follow you. For example, if you and a friend were picking players for a basketball game, and you could choose between me and LeBron James, it's clear who you'd pick: the guy who wins championships, not the guy who played basketball in high school more than fifty years ago! You want the guy who can produce and inspire his teammates to produce right along with him.

LEVEL 4: PEOPLE DEVELOPMENT

If you gain influence with your team on Levels 1, 2, and 3, people will consider you a fantastic leader. You will get a lot done, and you will be considered successful. But there are higher levels of leadership, because the greatest leaders do more than just get things done.

There are so many different kinds of leaders, both male and female. They come in all shapes and sizes, ages and degrees of experience, races and nationalities, from genius to average intelligence. What separates the good from the great?

Leaders become great not because of their power, but because of their ability to empower others. Success without a successor is ultimately failure. To create anything lasting, to develop a team or organization that can grow and improve, to build anything for the future, a leader's main responsibility is to develop other people: to help them reach their personal potential, to help them do their jobs more effectively, and to help

> Leaders become great not because of their power, but because of their ability to empower others.

them learn to become leaders themselves. This kind of people development leads to *reproduction*.

People development has a multiplying effect. Teams and organizations go to a whole new level when leaders begin developing others. One team develops enough leaders to create additional teams. One division, operation, or location develops enough leaders to create additional ones. Because everything rises and falls on leadership, having more and better leaders always leads to having a better organization.

The People Development level has another positive side effect: loyalty to the leader. People tend to be loyal to the mentor who helps improve their lives. If you watch a leader develop influence through the levels, you can see how the relationship progresses. On Level 1, the team member *has to follow* the leader. On Level 2, the team member *wants to follow* the leader. On Level 3, the team member *appreciates and admires* the leader because of what he or she has done for the team. On Level 4, the team member *becomes loyal* to the leader because of what the leader has done for him or her personally. You win people's hearts and minds by helping them grow personally.

> If you don't believe in the messenger, you won't believe the message.
>
> —JAMES M. KOUZES AND BARRY Z. POSNER

Not every good leader works to develop influence on Level 4. In fact, most leaders aren't even aware that Level 4 exists. They are so focused on their own productivity and that of their team that they don't realize they should be developing people. If that describes you, I want to help you. I've created some questions you should ask yourself about developing people that can help position you for success on Level 4:

1. Am I Passionate About My Personal Growth?

Only growing people are effective at growing others. If you still have that fire within you, people will feel it around you. I'm seventy years old, and I'm still fixated on growth.

2. Does My Growth Journey Have Credibility?

The first thing people ask themselves when you offer to help them grow is whether you have anything to offer that can help them. The key to that answer is your credibility. In their book *The Leadership Challenge*, James M. Kouzes and Barry Z. Posner expound on what they call the Kouzes-Posner First Law of Leadership: If you don't believe in the messenger, you won't believe the message. They go on to say of credibility, "Loyalty, commitment, energy, and productivity depend on it."[7]

3. Are People Attracted to Me Because of My Growth?

People want to learn from leaders they see growing and learning. One year at the Leadership Open, which my nonprofit organization EQUIP hosted at Pebble Beach, many people remarked about the incredible growth they were seeing in Mark Cole, my CEO. That kind of dramatic yet humble growth is very attractive to people.

4. Am I Successful in the Areas Where I Want to Develop Others?

You cannot give what you do not have. When I develop people, I try to help them primarily in areas where I'm successful: speaking, writing, and leadership. Do you know the areas where I never give advice? Singing. Technology. Golf. Nobody wants to hear what I have to say about these subjects. I'd be wasting their time and mine.

5. Have I Crossed Over the Spend Time / Invest Time Line?

Most people spend time *with* others. Few invest time *in* them. If you want to succeed at Level 4, you need to become an *investor* in people. This means adding value but also expecting to see a return on your investment— not in personal gain, but in impact. The return you're looking for is in people's personal growth, the betterment of their leadership, the impact of their work, the value they add to the team and organization. I learned this lesson at age forty when I realized my time was limited and I could not work any harder or longer than I already was. (I'll tell you more about this in chapter 2.) The only solution was to reproduce myself by investing in others. As they got better, the team got better. And so did I.

6. Do I Have a Teachable Way of Life?

Teachable people are the best teachers. To develop people, I need to remain teachable. That means wanting to learn, paying attention to what I learn, desiring to share what I learn, and knowing with whom to share it.

7. Am I Willing to Be a Vulnerable Role Model and Coach?

Developing people by investing in them doesn't mean pretending you have all the answers. It means being authentic, admitting what you don't know as much as what you do, and learning as much as you can from the people you're developing. Learning is a two-way street. Continuing to develop myself as I develop others brings me great joy.

8. Do the People I Develop Succeed?

The ultimate goal in developing people is to help them transform their lives. Teaching may help someone's life *improve*. True development helps an individual's life *change*. How can you tell if that's happened? The person you've invested in succeeds. Not only is that the greatest sign of transformation, it's the greatest reward to a leader who develops people.

How did you do? The more yeses you can honestly answer to the eight questions, the better you're positioned to develop people. If your noes outnumbered your yeses, don't lose heart. Make growth your goal to set you up for future success on Level 4. You won't regret it because this is where long-term success occurs. Your commitment to developing leaders will ensure ongoing growth in the organization, in the people you lead, and in your leadership impact. Do whatever you can to achieve and stay on this level.

LEVEL 5: PINNACLE

The final level of leadership is the Pinnacle. If you read the original version of this book, you may recall that I called this level *Personhood*. But I think *Pinnacle* is a more descriptive name. This highest level is based on *reputation*. This is rarified air. Only a few people reach this level. Those who do have led well and proven their leadership over a lifetime, have invested in other leaders and raised them up to Level 4, and have developed influence not only in their own organizations, but beyond them.

People at the Pinnacle level are known not only outside of their own organizations, but outside of their fields, their countries, and even their lifetimes. For example, Jack Welch is a Level 5 leader in business. Nelson Mandela was a Level 5 leader in government. Martin Luther King Jr. was a Level 5 leader among social activists. Leonardo da Vinci was a Level 5 leader in the arts and engineering. Aristotle was a Level 5 leader in education and philosophy.

Can everyone reach this level of leadership? No. Should we strive for it? Absolutely. But we shouldn't focus on it. Why? Because we can't manufacture respect in others, nor can we demand it. Respect must be freely given to us by others, so it's not within our control. For that reason, we should focus instead on developing influence on Levels 2, 3, and 4 and work hard to sustain it day after day, year after year, decade after decade. If we do that, we've done all we can do.

NAVIGATING THE LEVELS OF LEADERSHIP

I hope you can use the 5 Levels of Leadership as a clear visual reminder of how influence works. It's a paradigm *for* leadership and a pathway *to* leadership. Now that you can see the model, I want to give you a few insights that will help you not only to embrace it but to navigate using it as a leader:

- The 5 Levels of Leadership can be applied to every area of your life, both personal and professional.

- You are on a different level with each individual person in your life.
- Each time you add a level in your relationship with another person, your level of influence goes up.
- You never leave behind a previous level once you achieve a new one. The levels build and add to one another. They are not replaced.
- If you skip a level to try to speed up the process, you will have to circle back and earn that level anyway for the longevity of the relationship.
- The higher you go up the levels, the longer it takes.
- Each time you change jobs or join a new circle of people, you start on the lowest level and have to work your way up again.
- Once a level is earned, it must be maintained. No one ever "arrives" as a leader. Nothing is permanent in leadership.
- Just as you can add influence at a level, you can also lose influence at a level.
- It takes less time to lose a level than it does to earn it.

At this point in my life and career, the 5 Levels of Leadership have become second nature to me. As soon as I meet people, I begin working on the relationship. As soon as we've developed a connection, I try to add Production and achieve something together. And I begin looking for ways to add value to people and invest in them. I believe you can develop your influence in the same way I have. All it takes is will and intentionality.

I once read a poem called "My Influence." I don't know who the author is, but its message left an impact on me:

> My life shall touch a dozen lives
> Before this day is done,
> Leave countless marks for good or ill,
> Ere sets the evening sun;
> This is the wish I always wish,
> The prayer I always pray:
> Lord, may my life help other lives
> It touches by the way.[8]

If you're like me, you have goals. You want not only to achieve success, but also experience significance. You want your leadership to make a difference. The level you achieve is more dependent on your influence than on any other single factor. That's why influence is so important. You just don't know how many lives you'll touch. All you can do is develop your influence so that when opportunities come, you can make the best of them. Never doubt the power of one person of influence. Think of Aristotle. He mentored Alexander the Great, and Alexander conquered the world.

DEVELOPING THE *INFLUENCER* WITHIN YOU

One of the great challenges of applying the 5 Levels of Leadership is that you must earn each level of influence with every person in your life. While it's true that your level of influence with others is either increasing or decreasing every day, you will find it beneficial to focus your attention on intentionally increasing your influence with only a limited number of people at first.

For that reason, I suggest you pick two people in your life right now with whom to intentionally build your influence. Choose one important person from your professional life, maybe your boss, a key team member, a colleague, or a client. And choose one important person from your personal life, perhaps your spouse, your child, a parent, or a neighbor. (Yes, it is possible to be on only the Position level with your spouse or child, and yes, you have to earn—or re-earn—influence at the higher levels.) If you are a high-capacity person with lots of ambition and energy, you may choose *three* people.

First, determine which level of leadership you are currently on with each person. Then use the following guidelines to begin earning the level above your current one and to strengthen your influence at the lower levels.

Level 1: Position—Influence Based on Rights

- Know your role or job description thoroughly.
- Do your job with consistent excellence.
- Do more than expected.
- Accept responsibility for yourself and your leadership.
- Learn from every leadership opportunity.
- Be aware of the history that impacts personal dynamics.
- Don't rely on your position or title to help you lead.

Level 2: Permission—Influence Based on Relationship

- Value the other person.
- Learn to see through the other person's eyes by asking questions.
- Care more about the person than about the rules.
- Include the other person in your journey by shifting your focus from *me* to *we*.
- Make the other person's success your goal.
- Practice servant leadership.

Level 3: Production—Influence Based on Results

- Initiate and accept responsibility for your own personal growth.
- Develop accountability for results, beginning with yourself.
- Lead by example and produce results.
- Help the other person find and give his or her best contribution.

Level 4: People Development—Influence Based on Reproduction

- Embrace the idea that people are your most valuable asset.
- Be open and honest about your growth journey.
- Expose the other person to growth and leadership opportunities.
- Place the person in the best place to be successful.

Level 5: Pinnacle—Influence Based on Respect

- Focus your influence on the most promising 20 percent of the people you lead.
- Teach and encourage them to develop other high-level leaders.
- Leverage your influence to advance the organization.
- Use your influence outside the organization to make a difference.

If you would like additional help with the process of developing your leadership, please visit MaxwellLeader.com to receive free bonus materials I've created to help you. And be sure to take the free leadership self-assessment.

TWO

THE KEY TO LEADERSHIP:
PRIORITIES

Do you have plenty of time to do all that you want and need to do in a day? I'm guessing the answer is no. I have yet to meet any busy leaders who feel they have more than enough time to do all they want. In chapter 1 I mentioned that at age forty, I realized I alone couldn't work any harder or any longer, so I started investing in people. But I also realized that I needed to improve the way I managed myself and my time.

People used to talk a lot about time management, but the reality is that you can't manage time. Managing something means controlling it, changing it. When it comes to time, there is nothing to manage. Everybody gets twenty-four hours in a day. We can't add another hour or subtract one. We can't slow it down or speed it up. Time is what it is.

Coach and speaker Jamie Cornell wrote, "Time cannot and will not be managed, and you will never get more of it. The problem is rooted in the choices you are making with others and your own choices. You choose how to use it every moment of every day, whether you believe you do or not."[1]

For anyone who leads, the question is not, "Will my calendar be full?" but "Who and what will fill my calendar?" When I feel that I don't have enough time, I need to examine myself—my choices, my calendar, my *priorities*. These are the things we can control, not time. We need to determine how we will spend the twenty-four hours we have every day. That requires us to prioritize our time so we get more production out of those hours. That's especially true for leaders because our actions impact so many other people.

At a conference, I once heard a speaker say, "There are two things that are most difficult to get people to do: to think and to do things in order of importance." He was talking about priorities. Good leaders always think ahead and prioritize their responsibilities. It's been said that

- Practical people know how to get what they want.
- Philosophers know what they ought to want.
- Leaders know how to get what they ought to want.

That's why I want to help you identify what you ought to want as a leader—not according to my priorities but according to yours. And I want to help you follow through on those priorities effectively to enhance your life and improve your leadership.

PRIORITY PRESSURES

Nobody escapes the pressures of modern life, and because we all deal with demands, deadlines, and difficulties, we can get confused when it comes to our priorities. Here are some things I've found to be true:

MOST PEOPLE OVERESTIMATE THE IMPORTANCE OF MOST THINGS

Every day you could make a long list of things you want to do, ought to do, and have to do. Not all of them are important. Psychologist William James said, "The art of being wise is knowing what to overlook."[2] Petty and mundane tasks threaten to steal much of our time. If we're not careful, we can start living for the wrong things.

Having Too Many Priorities Paralyzes People

One of the most popular acts in circuses for many years was the performance of a lion tamer. The man or woman would walk into a cage full of dangerous lions and get them to do what he or she wanted. I once read there was a reason many of them would carry a stool or chair into the cage with them. Evidently, if the animal trainer held the chair by its back, with its legs facing the lion, the animal would try to focus on all four legs at once. This divided focus by the animal overwhelmed it, caused it to become paralyzed by indecision, and took away its aggression.

> The art of being wise is knowing what to overlook.
>
> —WILLIAM JAMES

That same kind of thing can happen to us. Just about all of us have experienced days when our to-do lists are long, our desks are piled with papers, our cell phones are ringing, and people come into our offices wanting something. If you're like most people, all these demands can freeze you up.

Years ago, one of our most productive staff members, Sheryl, came to see me. She looked exhausted. After we chatted, I learned that she felt totally overloaded by a massive list of responsibilities. I asked her to list all her tasks and projects. Then I went through them with her and prioritized them. The effect was immediate: it was as if a giant weight had been removed from her. I can still picture the look of relief on her face when she realized that she could focus on what mattered most and let the other things wait.

When Small Demands Are Given Too Much Attention, Big Problems Arise

Often the little things in life trip us up. A tragic example is the accident that occurred on Eastern Airlines flight 401 on the evening of December 29, 1971. The plane, carrying 163 passengers and 13 crew members out of New York, experienced a problem as it approached its destination in Miami. The light that indicates proper deployment of the landing gear failed to light. The pilot put the plane into a holding pattern while members of the flight crew tried to find out whether the landing gear was deployed.

The plane flew in a large, looping circle over the swamps of the Everglades while the cockpit crew checked to see if the gear actually had not deployed, or if instead the bulb in the signal light was defective. After some work, they removed the lightbulb, but they still weren't sure whether the landing gear was down. The pilot sent the second officer down into the avionic bay beneath the flight deck to try to ascertain whether the front wheel was down.

While the three experienced flight crew members were trying to chase down the problem, they lost track of something much more important: their altitude. While circling on autopilot, the plane had gradually lost altitude. Ten seconds after they noticed the problem, the plane flew right into the Everglades. Sadly, more than a hundred people died. And in the end, investigators discovered that the only problem was actually a faulty light bulb.

Robert J. McKain is said to have observed, "The reason most major goals are not achieved is that we spend our time doing second things first."[3] Or third things. Or fourth. Anytime small demands or insignificant tasks displace important tasks, we can get into trouble.

MAKING EVERYTHING A PRIORITY MEANS NOTHING IS A PRIORITY

A family that had become fed up with the noise and traffic of the city saved their money and finally realized their dream. They sold their cramped apartment, bought a ranch, and moved out west. Their desire was to move to the country to enjoy life in the wide-open spaces and raise cattle.

Some friends from the city came out to visit them a month later and asked them what they had named the ranch.

"Well," the new rancher said, "I wanted to call it the Flying W. But my wife said she wanted to call it the Suzy-Q. Our oldest thought the name should be the Bar-J, and our youngest hoped we would name it the Lazy Y. So we compromised. We're calling it the Flying Lazy Y-W-Bar-J Suzy-Q Ranch."

"Wow," said the friend. "Can I see your cattle?"

"We don't have any," the rancher replied. "None of them survived the branding!"

Okay, I'll admit it: that's a really corny joke, but I love it because it illustrates the fact that when you say *everything* is a high priority, then *nothing* is a high priority. It really indicates that you're unwilling or unable to make a decision, which means you won't get *anything* done.

SOMETIMES IT TAKES AN EMERGENCY TO FORCE PEOPLE TO PRIORITIZE

For some people, only a crisis can cause them to rethink their priorities. That was the case on the night of April 14, 1912, when the great ocean liner *Titanic* crashed into an iceberg in the Atlantic. One of the most curious stories to come from the disaster was of a woman who had a place in one of the lifeboats. At the last second, she asked if she could return to her stateroom for something. She was told she had only three minutes. As she hurried through the corridors, she stepped over money and other valuables where they had been dropped in haste. Once in her stateroom, she ignored her own jewelry and instead grabbed three oranges. Then she quickly returned to her place in the boat.

> When you say *everything* is a high priority, then *nothing* is a high priority.

Just hours earlier, she wouldn't have exchanged her least valuable piece of jewelry for a boxcar full of oranges, but circumstances had changed her priorities, as they can for many of us.

PRIORITY PRINCIPLES

Someone once said, "An infant is born with a clenched fist; an adult dies with an open hand. Life has a way of prying free the things we think are so important." If you want to develop the leader within you, don't wait for tragedy to realign your priorities. Become proactive about the process starting today. Begin by acknowledging the following principles:

1. Working Smarter Has a Higher Return Than Working Harder

Novelist Franz Kafka said, "Productivity is being able to do things that you were never able to do before." How do you make that happen? Doing the exact same things with greater intensity rarely works. As Albert Einstein allegedly pointed out, the definition of insanity is doing the same thing over and over and expecting different results.

> Disciplined use of the time everybody else wastes can give you the edge.
>
> —DAN KENNEDY

So how do you get better results? You have to *rethink* how you do something. You have to work smarter. That means finding better ways to work and making the most of the moments you have. Marketing expert Dan Kennedy says, "Disciplined use of the time everybody else wastes can give you the edge."[4] What leader doesn't want that?

2. You Can't Have It All

When my son, Joel, was a young child, every time we entered a store, I would have to tell him, "You can't have it all." Like many people, he had a hard time narrowing his want list. But I believe that 95 percent of achieving anything is knowing what you want. That's especially important for someone who is leading others.

Years ago I read a story about a group of people who were preparing for an ascent to the top of Mont Blanc in the French Alps. The evening before the climb, their French guide explained the main prerequisite for success. He said, "To reach the top, you must carry only what's necessary for climbing. You must leave behind all else. It's a very difficult climb."

A young Englishman disregarded the expert's advice, and the next morning he showed up with a bunch of items in addition to his equipment: a brightly colored blanket, large pieces of cheese, a bottle of wine, a couple of cameras with several lenses, and some bars of chocolate.

"You'll never make it with all that," said the guide. "You can only take the bare necessities to make the climb."

But the Englishman was young and strong-willed. He set off on his own in front of the group to prove that he could do it.

On the way up to the summit of Mont Blanc, the rest of the group, carrying only the necessities under the guide's direction, began to notice items along their path: first, there was a brightly colored blanket. Then a bottle of wine and some pieces of cheese. Camera equipment. And finally, chocolate bars.

When they reached the top, there was the Englishman. Wisely, he had jettisoned everything unnecessary along the way and had made the summit.

Many years ago I read a poem by William H. Hinson that communicates a great lesson about priorities:

> He who seeks one thing, and but one,
> May hope to achieve it before life is done.
> But he who seeks all things wherever he goes
> Must reap around him in whatever he sows
> A harvest of barren regret.

If you want to be successful as a person and as a leader, you must make choices. You must prioritize. You cannot have it all. No one can.

3. The Good Is Always the Enemy of the Best

Most people can prioritize between the good and the bad or between right and wrong. The real challenge arises when they are faced with two good choices. Which should they choose?

An excellent illustration of this can be found in a parable of a lighthouse keeper who worked on a rocky stretch of coastline before the days of electricity. Once a month he received a supply of oil to keep the light burning.

Not being far from town, he often had visitors. One night an old woman from the village begged for some oil to keep her family warm. He had pity on her and gave her oil. Another time a father asked for some oil for his lamp so that he could search for his missing son. Another person needed some oil to keep machinery going so that he and his employees could keep working. Each request was good, and each time, the lighthouse keeper gave them oil for their worthy cause.

Toward the end of the month, he noticed the supply of oil was very low. By the last night of the month, it was gone, and the beacon went out. That night in a storm, a ship wrecked on the rocks and lives were lost.

When the authorities investigated, the man was very repentant. But there was only one reply: "You were given oil for one purpose—to keep that light burning!"

As you become more successful and busier, you must learn to navigate the choice between two good things. You can't always have both. How do you choose? Remember that the good must sometimes be sacrificed for the best.

4. PROACTIVE BEATS REACTIVE

Every person is either an initiator or a reactor when it comes to planning. In my opinion you can choose or you can lose. Proactive means choosing. Reactive means losing. The question isn't "Will I have things to do?" but "Will I do things that make a difference?" To be an effective leader, you need to be proactive. Take a look at the difference between initiators and reactors:

Initiators	Reactors
Prepare	Repair
Plan ahead	Live in the moment
Pick up the phone and make contact	Wait for the phone to ring
Anticipate problems	React to problems
Seize the moment	Wait for the right moment
Put their priorities in their calendars	Put others' requests in their calendars
Invest time in people	Spend time with people

If you have any doubt about the impact of initiating versus reacting on your productivity, just think about the week before you go on vacation. It's probably your most productive and efficient time at work. Why?

Because you have clear priorities and a hard deadline. Before leaving the office for vacation, we need to make decisions, finish projects, clean off the desk, return calls, and close the loop with colleagues.

> You can choose or you can lose. Proactive means choosing. Reactive means losing.

Why can't we always run our lives that way? Actually, we can, but it requires a change in mind-set. Instead of focusing on efficiency, which is a survival mind-set, we need to think about effectiveness, which is a success mind-set. Instead of focusing on doing things right, we need to focus on doing only the right things. We need to become fervently and continuously proactive.

5. THE IMPORTANT NEEDS TO TAKE PRECEDENCE OVER THE URGENT

The more responsibility you carry as a leader, the more you have on your plate. The ability to juggle multiple high-priority projects successfully is something every successful leader must learn how to do. As the list of tasks grows, you can agonize or organize. I'd rather organize.

Here is a simple but effective way to classify tasks that can help you quickly prioritize them in any given moment. The goal is to determine how important the task is and how urgent it is. Ineffective leaders jump on the urgent tasks without thinking. Effective leaders weigh both factors for each task and act accordingly. Here's how:

- *High Importance/High Urgency:* Tackle these tasks first.
- *High Importance/Low Urgency:* Set deadlines for completion and fit these tasks into your daily routine.
- *Low Importance/High Urgency:* Find quick, efficient ways to get these tasks done with minimal personal involvement and time. If possible, delegate them.
- *Low Importance/Low Urgency:* If these tasks can be eliminated, then get rid of them. If they can be delegated, then find someone to do them. If you must do them, then schedule a one-hour block every week to chip away at them, but never schedule them during your prime time.

It doesn't take much time or effort to review your to-do list every morning and evaluate each task using the importance/urgency criteria. And it's an effective way to help you prioritize, put things into order quickly, and plan your day.

Having a strategy for evaluating your daily to-do list by priority is invaluable. After all, a life in which *anything goes* will ultimately be a life in which *nothing goes well*. But if you have no solutions for determining priorities other than that, you will still be too reactive instead of proactive as a leader. So I want to give you some tools that will help you with priorities in the bigger picture.

PROACTIVE PRIORITY SOLUTION #1:
THE PARETO PRINCIPLE

A veteran of many years of decision making gave me this simple and direct advice: decide what to do and do it; decide what not to do and don't do it. I love that, but the evaluation of priorities often isn't that simple. Many times, knowing what to do is not black or white, but many shades of gray.

Many years ago, while I was taking business courses, I was introduced to the Pareto principle, named for Italian economist Vilfredo Pareto. It is commonly called the 80/20 principle. I quickly saw the value of the concept and began applying it to my life. Forty-five years later, I still find it a most useful tool for determining priorities for myself, for anyone I coach, and for any organization. The Pareto principle, when applied to business, says:

> 20 percent of your priorities will give you 80 percent of your production, IF you spend your time, energy, money, and personnel on the top 20 percent of your priorities.

Here are some examples of how the Pareto principle plays out in life. Some of these are humorous, but all of them are true:

Time: 20 percent of our time produces 80 percent of our results
Counseling: 20 percent of the people take up 80 percent of our time

Products: 20 percent of the products bring in 80 percent of the profits

Books: 20 percent of the book contains 80 percent of the content

Jobs: 20 percent of our work gives us 80 percent of the satisfaction

Speeches: 20 percent of the presentation creates 80 percent of the impact

Donors: 20 percent of the donors give 80 percent of the money

Taxes: 20 percent of the people pay 80 percent of the taxes

Leadership: 20 percent of the people make 80 percent of the decisions

Picnics: 20 percent of the people will eat 80 percent of the food

Look at just about any situation, and you'll find that the 80/20 rule applies. Why? I don't know. It just does.

As a leader, you need to understand this principle, because it comes into play in everything you do as a leader. Visually, here's how the 80/20 rule looks if you have ten priorities:

The Pareto Principle

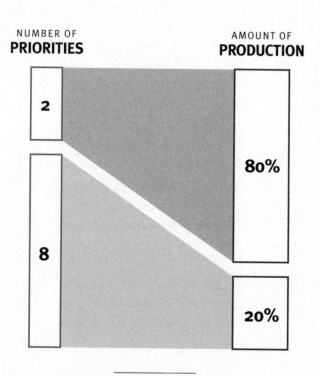

NUMBER OF
PRIORITIES

AMOUNT OF
PRODUCTION

2

8

80%

20%

The solid lines in the illustration represent your top two priorities. Spending time, energy, money, staff, and so forth on those two items would result in a fourfold return in productivity. However, the remaining eight items would give a minimal return.

The implications are clear: since the top 20 percent of the items on your to-do list give you an 80 percent return, you should focus on them. The top 20 percent of your staff give you an 80 percent return: focus your time and energy on them. The top 20 percent of your clients give you 80 percent of your return: focus on them. The top 20 percent of your offerings produce 80 percent of your return: focus on selling them.

The place this principle impacts leaders most is in the people they lead. Employees do not impact an organization equally. The top 20 percent carry the greatest load and make the greatest difference. Unfortunately, the people who require the most time and attention are often those in the bottom 20 percent. In contrast, the people at the top often demand the least from their leaders because they are motivated and self-directed. But who should you be taking time to invest in? The top 20 percent.

Here's how to apply the Pareto principle to the people on your team:

- Determine which people are the top 20 percent when it comes to production.
- Spend 80 percent of your people time with this top 20 percent.
- Spend 80 percent of your personal development dollars on this top 20 percent.
- Help the top 20 percent to determine what *their* top 20 percent return is, and allow them to give 80 percent of their time to it.
- Allow them to delegate the other 80 percent of their tasks to others to free them up for what they do best.
- Ask the top 20 percent to do on-the-job training for the next 20 percent.

How do you identify the top 20 percent on your team, in your department, or in your organization? I have provided a worksheet at the end of the chapter to help you do that. I strongly suggest that you take the time to use it because it's critical that you invest in your top 20 percent.

If there are five people on your team, your number one person is your top 20 percent. If ten, then the first and second on the list. If twenty, then the top four. You get the idea. Your top 20 percent are the people you should be investing in, giving resources to, and providing with leadership opportunities. They will make or break the team.

PROACTIVE PRIORITY SOLUTION #2:
THE THREE RS

If you are from my generation, you remember teachers talking about the three Rs: reading, 'riting, and 'rithmetic. (I know—two of the three Rs don't even start with R!) I want to offer you a different three Rs to help you become highly proactive in identifying and living your priorities. To do that, you have to look at your life from a bigger-picture perspective. Think of it as a thirty-thousand-foot perspective. The three Rs are *requirement*, *return*, and *reward*. (See, they actually start with R.) You can discover your major priorities by asking yourself three questions based on these three Rs:

WHAT IS REQUIRED OF ME?

Every role has responsibilities that are nonnegotiable. There are things you must do that you cannot delegate to anyone else. Do you know what they are? When I became the leader of Skyline Church in San Diego, I asked the board who was hiring me, "What must I do that only I can do and cannot delegate to anyone else?" We talked it through for a couple of hours. They decided there were only a few things only I could do, such as being the primary communicator most Sundays, carrying the vision of the church, and maintaining my personal integrity. These were my nonnegotiables and could be fulfilled by no one but me.

In the end a leader can give up anything except final responsibility. If you work for a boss or a board, they can help you answer the requirement question. If you work for yourself or you own your own business, the question may be more difficult to answer. But it's critical. Otherwise, you'll end up focusing on the wrong things, which could waste your time, talent, and energy.

What Gives Me the Greatest Return?

What are you good at? I mean, really good at? This is at the heart of the return question. What brings the greatest return on your investment of time and energy for your organization? That's a question I continually ask myself. I understand that activity is not accomplishment, productivity is. I'm at my most productive using my best talents, gifts, and experience doing three things: communicating, writing, and leading. Those give the greatest return to me and to my organizations. They are my sweet spot. Anything else I do is second-rate—or worse.

Activity is not accomplishment, productivity is.

Knowing what activities give you the greatest return is vital. What do people continually compliment you for doing? What tasks or responsibilities do colleagues continually ask you to take on? What do you do that makes the biggest positive impact or brings in the most revenue? These are clues to help you answer the return question.

What Is Most Rewarding?

Life is too short not to be fun. Our best work is accomplished when we enjoy it. It gives us great internal rewards, which can be mental, emotional, or spiritual. And here's the standard I often teach to help people answer the reward question. Find something you like to do so much that you would gladly do it for nothing. Then learn to do it so well that people are happy to pay you for it. Here's a clue for knowing what's most rewarding. When you do something and you think to yourself, *I was born for this*, you're on the right track.

Your long-term career goal should be to align the tasks that answer your requirement, return, and reward questions. If what you must do, what you do well, and what you enjoy doing are all the same things, then your career priorities are in sync and you will live a productive and fulfilling life. It takes time and hard work to bring those things together. At the end of this chapter, I have provided a road map to help you evaluate how you're currently doing with your three Rs so that you can start working to get them into alignment.

PROACTIVE PRIORITY SOLUTION #3:
MAKE ROOM FOR MARGIN

For years I've practiced the discipline of spending a few hours during the last week of the month planning out my time schedule for the upcoming month. I would literally schedule my priorities and requirements into hourly time blocks, day by day. And I used to pride myself on how I valued and prioritized my time. I had mistakenly convinced myself that if I could keep to the schedule and work fast and long enough, I would get to a place where I was caught up on everything. And that would create margin in my life.

After years of this fruitless exercise, I discovered that I was deceiving myself. I realized that Parkinson's law is true: work expands so that it fills the time available for its completion. Unless I did something intentional to create margin, I would never have it in my life.

Physician and author Richard Swenson has written extensively on the idea of margin. In his book *Margin: Restoring Emotional, Physical, Financial, and Time Reserves to Overloaded Lives*, he wrote, "Margin is the space that exists between our load and our limits. It is the amount allowed beyond that which is needed. It is something held in reserve for contingencies or unanticipated situations. Margin is the gap between rest and exhaustion, the space between breathing freely and suffocating. Margin is the opposite of overload."[5]

Instead of filling every space in my calendar, what I needed to do was create some white space. If I didn't, nobody else was going to. People who keep burning the candle at both ends aren't as bright as they think they are. I needed to change by creating margin in my life.

> Margin is the space that exists between our load and our limits.
>
> —RICHARD SWENSON

In *The 21 Irrefutable Laws of Leadership*, I wrote about the Law of Priorities, which says, "Leaders understand that activity is not necessarily accomplishment."[6] Even though I wrote about that law, I must confess that living it has been a continual challenge for me for more than twenty years. Creating margin is not easy for a person who loves to work, thrives on deadlines, and continually feels the press to make things happen. But I also recognize that the greater the responsibilities you have as a leader, the more responsible you are to create margin in your life.

By no means do I follow through with this perfectly, but I *do* work persistently to create margin in my life. If you desire to be a leader who lives according to your priorities and reach your potential, then you need to learn how to create margin too. Here's why:

1. Margin Improves Self-Awareness

Emotional intelligence (EQ) is the ability to recognize and understand emotions in yourself and others, and to apply this awareness so that you manage your behavior and your relationships with others. There are few abilities more important than EQ when it comes to leadership. The training and consulting organization TalentSmart has tested more than a million people for EQ and found that 90 percent of top performers rate high in EQ.[7]

One of the fantastic things about EQ is that, like leadership, it can be developed. A foundational characteristic of EQ is self-awareness. A strong recognition and understanding of your own emotions can be developed during times of reflection, often when you're alone. Those windows of time don't come if you're overloaded and never have time for self-reflection. Margin creates such times, which provides you with the opportunity to grow in your EQ.

2. Margin Gives You Needed Think Time

Most leaders I've met have a strong bias for action. I know that's true of me. But if I spend all my time acting and never thinking about what I'm doing, I won't be a very effective leader. When I lead others, it's my responsibility to try to see more and before others see. I have to think more and before the people I'm leading. Truett Cathy, the founder of Chick-fil-A, told me, "We need to be thought leaders before we can be market doers." Creating margin lets us do that.

It is true that we are today where our thoughts have brought us, and we will go tomorrow where our thoughts take us. That's why I'm dedicated to reflective thinking and have written about it in so many of my books. If you want to become a good thinker, you need to create white space in your calendar for it, not just settle for a minute here and a few seconds there. You need to schedule significant blocks of time for it. If you're constantly running from one to-do or appointment to the next from sunup to sundown, you'll never become a better thinker.

3. Margin Provides You with Energy Renewal

We live in a culture of busyness, and leaders are often the busiest people of all. Founder and CEO of the Energy Project, Tony Schwartz, has studied and written extensively on energy and performance. He wrote in a *New York Times* article, "More and more of us find ourselves unable to juggle overwhelming demands and maintain a seemingly unsustainable pace." His solution? "Paradoxically," he said, "the best way to get more done may be to spend more time doing less. A new and growing body of multidisciplinary research shows that strategic renewal—including daytime workouts, short afternoon naps, longer sleep hours, more time away from the office, and longer, more frequent vacations—boosts productivity, job performance and, of course, health."[8]

> If you're constantly running from one to-do or appointment to the next from sunup to sundown, you'll never become a better thinker.

All of the things Schwartz described as beneficial require margin. And he said that human beings are designed not to expend high energy continuously, but to alternate between spending energy and recovering energy. So if you want to be at your best, you need to find ways to recharge. You can do that by creating space for relationships, exercise, recreation, travel, music, and so on. Whatever recharges your personal batteries is good. But you need to find margin for it.

HOW TO CREATE MARGIN

As I've said, creating margin is a challenge for me. But I keep fighting for it because I know it helps me live out my priorities and be a better leader. Here are two things I do that I believe can help you too.

Evaluate and Eliminate Continually

I'm constantly on the lookout for ways to simplify my life. I try not to spend time on things that are out of my sweet spot. I delegate or dump anything that doesn't fit into the three Rs. And I use the 80/20 principle whenever possible to downsize. You can too. Start by asking yourself some of the following questions:

- What are the 20 percent of my possessions I get the most value out of?
- What are the 20 percent of the clothes I wear 80 percent of the time?
- What do I spend 20 percent of my leisure time doing that gives me 80 percent of my happiness?
- Who are the 20 percent of the people I'm close to who make me the happiest?

Chances are you answered all of these questions fairly easily. You've just never considered looking at these areas in this way before. Focus on the areas where you gain the most. In the remainder, create margin. Give away clothes or possessions. Reduce the complexity of your life.

Fight to Keep 20 Percent of Your Calendar as White Space

My days of automatically filling up my calendar with tasks are done. Instead, I schedule white space into my calendar. With a nod to Pareto, my target is always to leave 20 percent of my time free. I would suggest that you fight for that same percentage.

What might that look like? You could choose to create margin every day. If you spend on average sixteen hours a day awake, creating margin means leaving three hours and twelve minutes unscheduled every day. If you wanted to think in terms of your week, you would need to leave about twenty-two and a half hours unscheduled every week. Margin by the month: leave six days totally open. By the year: seventy-two unscheduled days.

You may be saying to yourself, "I can't do that. I can't spare three hours a day or six days a month. And I'm definitely not taking more than seventy days off!" I think the same way. That's why margin is so difficult to maintain. Tony Schwartz agrees: "Taking more time off is counterintuitive for most of us. The idea is also at odds with the prevailing work ethic in most companies, where downtime is typically viewed as time wasted. More than one-third of employees, for example, eat lunch at their desks on a regular basis. More than 50 percent assume they'll work during their vacations."[9]

Yet to create margin, taking essential time off is exactly what we need to learn how to do. You can't maintain your priorities if you fill your life with busyness.

If you're a high-energy doer, you may find it difficult to stop, take stock of your activities, think through your priorities, and reevaluate what you do and how you do it. But you need to do it—not just once but day after day, year after year. Priorities never stay put. Yet if you can learn to master the principles of priorities and you develop the discipline of applying them continually, you will find your personal and professional effectiveness will be off the charts. Few things give a leader as great a return as good priorities. That's why I say they are the key to leadership.

Priorities never stay put.

DEVELOPING THE *PRIORITIZER* WITHIN YOU

The need to get a handle on priorities can feel overwhelming, especially in our culture, where busyness is expected and being overloaded is applauded. For that reason you may want to do this chapter's application in stages.

EMBRACE PRIORITY PRINCIPLES

Begin by determining the areas where you've not lived according to good priorities. Think about how you can change your everyday work habits. Answer the following five questions based on the priority principles in the chapter:

1. Where do I need to work smarter instead of harder?
2. What must I change to stop trying to have it all?
3. What good things can I stop doing in order to do the best?
4. What must I do to become more proactive instead of reactive?
5. What can I do to stop doing urgent but unimportant things?

PARETO PRINCIPLE WORKSHEET

The Pareto principle can be applied to almost any area of your personal or professional life. For leaders, the most critical application comes in your investment in people. You need to identify the top 20 percent of the people you lead.

1. Write the names of everyone on your team in the spaces below.

ABC	#	Name

2. In the far left column beside each name, write one of the following letters to complete this sentence: *This person leaving the team or working against me . . .*

   a. Could make or break the team, and it would greatly impact our effectiveness. (My friend Bill Hybels says that when you even think about losing one of these people, you feel like you're going to throw up.)

   b. Would negatively impact our effectiveness, but it would not break the team.

   c. Would not negatively affect the team, and it might even improve it.

   Every name should now have a letter beside it.

3. Now rank the importance of your A's by writing a 1 by the name of the most impacting person, a 2 next to the next most impacting, and so on. Then rank your Bs. Then your Cs.

4. Place an asterisk (*) next to the names of your top 20 percent (one name if you have a total of five on your list, two names if you have ten, etc.)

5. On another piece of paper, list two to five ways you can add value to those top people and develop them.

6. Look at anyone you marked with a C. If you have the authority, try to help these individuals find a place on another team where they might be more effective.

THREE Rs WORKSHEET

List your responsibilities on the next page. Then use each column to evaluate them. Beginning with the "Requirement" column, score them with either a 3 (high importance), 2 (moderate importance), or 1 (low importance). Then do the same for the "Return" and "Reward" columns. Once you've created ratings for every item in all three columns, add the scores. Based on the scores, rank your responsibilities in order using the far left column.

#	Responsibilities	Rqrmt	Return	Reward	Results
					=
					=
					=
					=
					=
					=
					=
					=
					=
					=
					=
					=
					=
					=
					=
					=
					=
					=

When you're done, you may have something that looks like this:

Responsibilities	Rqrmt	Return	Reward	Results
New Client Acquisition	3	3	2	= 8
Closing Deals with Clients	3	3	3	= 9
Answering E-mails	1	1	1	= 3
Supervision of Staff	3	2	1	= 6
Leadership Development of Staff	1	3	3	= 7
Project Oversight	2	2	2	= 6
Monthly Reports	3	1	1	= 5

Look at the responsibilities with your highest scores. Then assess whether your daily activities are aligned based on them. Don't just dismiss this question. Give it some thinking time. And if you're not sure about the answer, ask a friend, family member, or colleague who is willing to be honest with you. Once you've made the assessment, write a game plan for aligning your life with your priorities.

Margin Call

Examine your calendar. How much white space does it contain? If it contains less than 20 percent, you need to begin doing some cutting. (If you don't use a calendar of any kind, then start using one today. You have a different kind of problem with priorities.) Use the work you've already done in this chapter as your guide concerning what to cut and what to keep.

THREE

THE FOUNDATION OF LEADERSHIP:
CHARACTER

On October 12, 2016, I had the privilege of meeting Pope Francis and spending a few minutes with him. I have admired him for many years. His humility and character have made a strong impression on me. Traditionally, when a cardinal is newly elected as pope, when asked if he will accept his election, he responds, "*Accepto*," meaning "I accept." Francis's first words were instead, "I am a great sinner, but I trust in the infinite mercy and patience of our Lord Jesus Christ, and I accept in a spirit of penance."[1]

This man has led the way toward championing character formation within the leadership of the church. And his heart for transformation stirred me to ask him to pray for the John Maxwell Foundation, the nonprofit organization I founded to become a catalyst for positive transformation in countries such as Guatemala and Paraguay. I was humbled when he said yes.

CHARACTER IN LEADERSHIP

In the lead-up to my meeting with the pontiff, I read a lot about him. One of the articles I came across was by Gary Hamel, a management consultant and founder of Strategos, in the *Harvard Business Review*. Hamel wrote about a meeting Pope Francis had with a group of church leaders in which he outlined the problems inherent in leadership. He called them "diseases." There were fifteen of them, and most of them dealt with character:

1. *Thinking we are immortal, immune, or downright indispensable*—which is the enemy of humility and service.
2. *Excessive busyness*—which leads to stress and agitation.
3. *Mental and [emotional] "petrification"*—which creates heartlessness.
4. *Excessive planning and functionalism*—which leads to inflexibility.
5. *Poor coordination*—which fosters independence and lack of cooperation.
6. *"Leadership Alzheimer's disease"*—where leaders forget who nurtured and mentored them.
7. *Rivalry and vainglory*—where titles and perks become leaders' primary focus.
8. *Existential schizophrenia*—where leaders live hypocritical double lives.
9. *Gossiping, grumbling, and backbiting*—where cowardly leaders speak ill of others behind their backs.
10. *Idolizing superiors*—where leaders honor superiors to gain favor and get ahead.
11. *Indifference to others*—where leaders think only of themselves.
12. *Downcast faces*—where leaders treat their "inferiors" with sour severity.
13. *Hoarding*—which involves accumulating material goods to seek security.
14. *Closed circles*—where leaders place their clique ahead of shared identity and cooperation.
15. *Extravagance and self-exhibition*—where leaders seek greater power and recognition.[2]

I found this list quite insightful. It's clear that Pope Francis has dealt with all kinds of leaders during a long career of service. And the list prompted me to examine my own character. *Am I a healthy leader?* I wondered. I read a list of questions included in the article that were designed to help with the self-examination process, which asked, to what extent do I . . .

Feel superior to those who work for me?
Demonstrate an imbalance between work and other areas of life?
Substitute formality for true human intimacy?
Rely too much on plans and not enough on intuition and
    improvisation?
Spend too little time breaking silos and building bridges?
Fail to regularly acknowledge the debt I owe to my mentors and to
    others?
Take too much satisfaction in my perks and privileges?
Isolate myself from customers and first-level employees?
Denigrate the motives and accomplishments of others?
Exhibit or encourage undue deference and servility?
Put my own success ahead of the success of others?
Fail to cultivate a fun and joy-filled work environment?
Exhibit selfishness when it comes to sharing rewards and praise?
Encourage parochialism rather than community?
Behave in ways that seem egocentric to those around me?[3]

Questions like these heighten my awareness of the need to keep improving my character, especially in the context of leadership, because the heightened influence of leaders magnifies their impact on others—both positively and negatively. The reality is that leading ourselves is often the most difficult task we face every day. It's much easier to tell others what to do than to do it ourselves. I know that's true of me.

To keep myself on track, I must continually remind myself why character is so important. Since I am a person of faith, I have discovered wisdom from Scripture related to character. I found the following list in David Kadalie's *Leader's Resource*

> The reality is that leading ourselves is often the most difficult task we face every day.

Kit. If you don't connect with these thoughts or are offended by them, please feel free to skip past them.

- Our hearts can be deceptive (Jeremiah 17:9; Psalm 139:23, 24).
- We can so easily seek leadership office for the wrong reasons (Matthew 20:17–28).
- Character is the area that will face the greatest attack (Romans 7; Galatians 5:16–24).
- Character is foundational to Christian leadership (1 Timothy 3:1–13; Titus 1:6–9).
- Without it we struggle with the temptations that come with skill, talents and gifting (Romans 12:3–8).
- It is so easy to slip into a life of hypocrisy and forget that we will have to give an account one day (Hebrews 4:13).
- We naturally neglect this part and focus on other developments (1 Timothy 4:7–8).
- We soon discover that strength of character is what will count in hard times (2 Corinthians 4:16–17).[4]

Working on my character is a never-ending yet totally worthwhile effort. Mahatma Gandhi said, "A man of character will make himself worthy of any position he is given." I want to be a worthy leader, yet I know I sometimes fall short. I want to improve my character—and encourage you to improve yours—not because it gets me what I want, but because it helps me to *be* what I want. And I find that the more I focus on valuing people, practicing self-leadership, and embracing good values, the stronger my character becomes.

CHARACTER VALUE STATEMENTS

Having good character does not ensure that you will be successful in life or leadership. But you can be sure that having poor character will eventually derail you personally and professionally. But here's the good news: if your character is not what you want it to be, you can change it. It doesn't matter what has happened in your past. You can choose a better path moving forward, starting today. As one of my favorite sayings goes, "Though you cannot go back and make a brand-new start, my friend, anyone can start from now and make a brand-new end."

Here are three great reasons why good character is worth pursuing:

1. Good Character Builds Strong Trust

Recently I asked a small group of executives to list the names of the top three people they trusted. Family and friends were on everyone's list. Amazingly, no one named a leader or a coworker as one of their top trusted people.

I then asked them to list three people on whom their well-being and happiness depended. Everyone named either their boss or a coworker.

Then I asked one more question: "If I were doing this exercise with *your* subordinates, and I asked them to create their 'most trusted' list, would they name you as one of their three most trusted people?" There was a murmur. That got their attention. "What difference might it make if you were someone they put on their list?"

The consensus was that if people trusted their coworkers and leaders, the working environment would be more positive, people would be more productive, and turnover would be reduced. That's consistent with my own observation that people quit people, not companies. The greatest cause of turnover in organizations is lack of trust.

Stephen M. R. Covey in his book *The Speed of Trust* pointed out how low trust costs time and money, and he used a fantastic example to illustrate it. After the 9/11 terrorist attacks, the nation's trust in flight security went down. Covey said that before the attacks, he could arrive at his home airport thirty minutes before his flight and have no problem making it quickly through security. However, after the TSA tightened security, he had to arrive two hours ahead of domestic flight departures and three hours ahead for international flights. "As trust went down," he said, "speed also went down and cost went up."[5]

Too often we talk about trust as if it is a singular thing. It is not. Trust is a relationship between a trustor and a trustee. Just as it takes two to tango, it takes two to trust. The role of the trustor is to take the risk of trusting; the role of the trustee is to be trustworthy. When both people do their parts well, the result is a trusting relationship.

And trust doesn't just go in one direction. The people exchange roles, the trustee becoming the trustor, and vice versa. It's a two-way street. But if either party fails in his or her responsibility, trust disappears.

Authors James M. Kouzes and Barry Z. Posner explain the importance of the development of trust in leaders:

> In the final analysis only you can decide whether to take the risk of trusting others and whether the risks are worth taking. This means to have others trust you, you must actively take some initiative and can't wait for others to make the first move. As many leaders explained, "Trust is a risk game. Leaders must be the first ones to ante-up." Leaders always find the ante worth risking. Sowing seeds of trust with people creates the fields of collaboration necessary to get extraordinary things done in organizations.[6]

For years I have taught leaders that in their interactions with others they create "accounts" of trustworthiness. Every interaction with another person either makes deposits in that person's account or makes withdrawals from it. The best way to make regular ongoing deposits is by modeling good character consistently. Why? Because people are convinced more by what a leader does than by what a leader says. I find myself agreeing with the idea expressed by industrialist and philanthropist Andrew Carnegie, who said, "As I grow older I pay less attention to what men say. I just watch what they do." Words can be cheap. Journalist Arthur Gordon was right when he said, "Nothing is easier than saying words. Nothing is harder than living them, day after day. What you promise today must be renewed and re-decided tomorrow and each day that stretches out before you." That's why in leadership a pint of example equals a gallon of advice.

> Trust is a risk game. Leaders must be the first ones to ante-up.
>
> —JAMES M. KOUZES AND BARRY Z. POSNER

In the beginning of a relationship, words hold more weight than actions. Because people do not know you, they may assume that your words represent who you are and that your walk matches your talk. However, as the relationship continues, your actions begin to weigh more than your words. People see what you do. Leadership confusion occurs when your words and your walk do

> In leadership a pint of example equals a gallon of advice.

not match. If that incongruity continues, not only will you confuse your people—you will lose your people. Mark Twain was right-on when he said, "To do right is wonderful. To teach others to do right is even more wonderful—and much easier." Easier? Yes. More effective? No.

At the opposite end of the spectrum from inconsistency and broken trust is moral authority. This is the highest level of leadership. It is earned by demonstrating consistently good character and continually making deposits into trustworthiness accounts with others. Charisma may get leaders a following early on, but only credibility prompts people to keep following them. When leaders possess true moral authority, the only words they need to say are "Follow me," and people join them. They know that their walk matches their talk and is headed in the right direction. Can we all gain moral authority as leaders? Maybe not. But we should strive to do our best to develop and display good character so that we are at least candidates to develop it.

I have to confess, my view on character and moral authority has changed over the years. I used to see trust as black or white. Now that I'm older, I've grown. And I think I have greater insight into how trust works and how character comes into play with it. I'd like to share with you some of the changes I've had in my thinking. See if you agree with them. Maybe you will, maybe you won't. That's okay. Another good thing about getting older is that I'm very comfortable with people not always agreeing with me.

I Thought Trust Was "Nice to Have"

Early in my leadership journey, I didn't recognize the importance of trust. I thought it was nice to have. Who doesn't want to be trusted, given the choice? But now I understand that in leadership, trust is essential. It's not something you can take or leave. If you leave trust, you're going to leave leadership.

Trust dramatically impacts real leadership issues, such as follower engagement, connection, buy-in, and effectiveness. Trust is the foundation of leadership. A strong foundation isn't a luxury. It's not just "nice to have." It's critical.

I Thought Trust Was Up to Others

Some leaders, especially those who rely on their position or title to lead instead of on their influence, take the posture that they should be implicitly trusted by their people, but that their people must prove themselves to be trustworthy. They put all the burden for developing trust on others, not themselves. But developing trust is a leadership responsibility. If I want to be a good leader, it's not up to my followers; it's up to me. I must take the first step in trusting the people I lead. And I must take steps to earn their trust. Good leaders take the risk in both directions. If my people learn to trust me, I'll get their attention. But if I initiate trust in my people, I'll get their action. And the essence of successful leadership is getting things done.

> If my people learn to trust me, I'll get their attention. But if I initiate trust in my people, I'll get their action.

I Thought Trust Could Only Grow Slowly

While it's true that trust often does grow slowly, it doesn't always have to work that way. For example, when individuals you trust vouch for someone they trust, you're likely to give this new person the benefit of the doubt and trust him or her. Why? Because of the relationship you have with your trusting friend. You transfer your trust—at least until you discover reasons of your own to withdraw that trust.

Another instance where trust can be earned quickly comes when someone performs an unselfish act of significance for another person. I experienced this as a young leader when another leader stuck up for me at a crucial time. His endorsement of me in a meeting gained me favor with others. I was grateful, because I had done nothing to earn it, and he could gain nothing for himself by giving it. He immediately gained my trust.

Here's an encouraging thought. We can be the person who does something selfless for others and helps them along their way. Doing this makes the world a better place. And if we do it for the people we lead and help them become more successful with no ulterior motives, we can develop a relationship of trust rapidly.

I Thought a Single Mistake Automatically Destroyed Trust

While it's true that a single mistake can destroy trust, that is not always the case. When the trust level is already low, then that's often all it takes. However, if the trust level is high, one mistake seldom destroys what people have built in the relationship.

If you're as old as I am, you remember the days of President Nixon and Watergate. Immediately after the scandal broke, the trust level was very low toward leaders in the United States. At that time, I remember hearing Billy Graham, whom I greatly respect, say, "Everybody has a little bit of Watergate in him." That was level-setting. It brought a dose of reality to everyone's idealism regarding leaders. If someone like Billy Graham has a little bit of Watergate in him, then so do I. And so do you.

Always doing right regardless of the situation goes against our nature. But we can fight to do what's right most of the time. And we can know that as long as we keep adding deposits to our trustworthiness accounts with others, we have a chance to withstand the mistakes we do make. Knowing this allows me to forgive my humanness as a leader. And it helps me be more committed to extending grace to other leaders when they make mistakes in their humanness.

I have a much longer view of character now than I did years ago. I recognize that character development is a lifelong process. In his book *Build Your Reputation*, networking expert Rob Brown described this ongoing process.

In the world of work and business, your "go-to" status won't happen overnight. It won't even happen by chance. You're building a platform here. A house if you like. Brick by brick. Comment by comment. Conversation by conversation. Even if you could build it fast, how sturdy would it be? . . .

You don't want to be a one-hit wonder. Any fool can get hired or booked once. The best, most sought-after thought leaders and prime promotional candidates didn't start out yesterday. It's a slog. It means some heavy lifting. It's going to take a little time. And it's going to be so worth it! . . .

But be under no illusions, building a great reputation requires a consistent, focused effort. Tortoise and the hare. Slow and steady wins the race. Marathon, not a sprint, and all that. With a few spurts here and there.[7]

So much of leadership relies on good character. Trust is created through it. Talent is protected by it. Internal peace is fostered by it. People cannot climb beyond the limitations of their character. Leaders cannot succeed beyond the depth of their character. Good leaders have the potential to be difference makers, and character makes a difference for them and protects them. Good leaders are often a gift to the world. Character protects that gift.

2. Successful Leaders Embrace the Four Dimensions of Character

In his book *Derailed*, Tim Irwin wrote that there are four dimensions to character: *authenticity, self-management, humility,* and *courage*.[8] I agree with his perspective and I want to use those four dimensions as my framework for describing the process of character building. Let's look at each of them:

Authenticity

I've observed that a lot of leaders have a difficult time with authenticity. Many don't want to let down their guard. They may feel that they are in a no-win situation. They worry that if they reveal their failures, they'll lose credibility. Yet if they try to hide their failures, they come across as phony. If they hide their successes, they fear they won't have as much credibility. But if they highlight only their successes, they come across as arrogant and unrelatable. How does a leader navigate this situation?

My advice to leaders is to try to live between the lines. Let me explain. As I travel the road of leadership, to my right is the line of success. When I'm over near that line, everything is going well, I'm achieving success, and I'm winning. To my left is the line of failure. When I'm close to that line, nothing seems to go right, and I'm living Murphy's Law: anything that can go wrong will go wrong, and at the worst possible time. I describe these two extremes this way:

> There are four dimensions to character: authenticity, self-management, humility, and courage.

The Line of Failure	The Line of Success
Weakness	Strength
Depresses me	Impresses me
I want no one to see	I want everyone to see
I want this never	I want this forever
Me at my worst	Me at my best

Most of the time we live between those two lines. When people see us on the success line, we have to be careful not to think that is who we really are. We can be like the athlete who wins a gold medal or a Super Bowl and starts to believe he's spectacular all the time at everything he does. It's not reality. People may try to put such individuals on a pedestal, but they will surely fall off.

There are also times when we travel along the failure line. We all make mistakes. We all make bad choices. We all fall short. If we believe that's who we are, we won't want to get out of bed. We shouldn't buy into that either. Both lines—of success and of failure—are extremes. We're neither as good nor as bad as they might indicate.

Authenticity is about living an open life between those lines. In my early years, I only wanted to tell others about my experiences on the success line. I wanted to impress people. As I grow older, I feel an opposite pull to share my failures so that I can encourage people. Because I'm a public figure, people often only see me at my best, not my worst. For that reason, some people give me more credit than I deserve. That bothers me. Instead of wanting to point to my breakthroughs, I want to direct people to the *brokenness* that has *led* to my breakthroughs.

I like to think of myself as a mosaic, made of many broken pieces. Author and blogger Rosalina Chai wrote a beautiful piece about mosaics that I find insightful.

> Mosaic is at once intricate yet majestic. And it is precisely its brokenness that lends mosaic its perception of fragile beauty. . . . And isn't this true too of our humanity? . . . What is it about brokenness that we find so offensive?
>
> What would happen when we accept and embrace that being broken is an essential part of humanity's be-ing? What would happen when we cease to label brokenness as bad? What would it take for us to cease labeling brokenness as bad? I can imagine one certainty . . . more peace.
>
> Accepting and embracing brokenness is not the same as using another's brokenness to feel better about ourselves. Rather, it is an acknowledgment of our common humanity. When I accept my own brokenness, and do not judge myself harshly because of it, I find myself capable of more compassion towards others regardless of whether I am aware of the form of brokenness they've experienced.[9]

Wholeness does not mean perfection. It means embracing brokenness as an integral part of our lives. My friend Max Lucado says, "God would rather us walk with an occasional limp than a continual strut." I am learning to embrace my limp because I'm learning so much.

> God would rather us walk with an occasional limp than a continual strut.
>
> —MAX LUCADO

None of us is flawless. Good people do bad things. Smart people do dumb things. We all find ourselves in moments where we feel tempted to do something we know in our hearts isn't the right thing, and we've all veered off course. It's humbling. Sharing that with others is authentic.

Self-Management

Author and speaker Ruth Haley Barton says, "We set young leaders up for a fall if we encourage them to envision what they can do before they consider the kind of person they should be." What she's speaking about is the strengthening of character that comes from good self-management.

Character is not about intelligence. It's about making right choices. David Gergen, the political commentator who worked in several White House administrations, points out that if intelligence and character were the same things, presidents Nixon and Clinton would have been two of the best. Gergen said, "Capacity counts, but once a candidate passes that test, character counts even more."[10]

> We set young leaders up for a fall if we encourage them to envision what they can do before they consider the kind of person they should be.
>
> —RUTH HALEY BARTON

Many leaders score high on IQ but low on CQ—character quotient. To increase our CQ we need to practice self-management. One of the best ways to help ourselves do that is to establish character guardrails for ourselves to keep us from going off course. On a highway, guardrails keep cars from going over a cliff. With them in place, you may crash, but you likely won't die.

When it comes to character, I believe the best guardrails are the decisions you make *before* you face high-pressure situations. It's easier to manage yourself if you've already made the tough decisions related to your values. It's impossible to maintain good character when you don't know what you value. Do you value honesty and integrity? Then what is your guardrail? What *won't* you do? Decide that before you face temptation. Do you value relationships? If so, what is your guardrail? What *must* you do to maintain relationships? Identify your values and decide what boundaries you won't cross long before you may be tempted to cross them.

I wrote about this concept in my book *Today Matters.* Many of the value decisions I've made were settled when I was in my teens and twenties. But I still have to manage myself in areas where I'm vulnerable to character pitfalls. For example, when you get to be my age and you've experienced some level of success, people start to give you honors and awards. I can't allow any of that to go to my head. My mentor Fred Smith taught me that the gift is greater than the person, meaning that a person may accomplish much, even though he or she is highly flawed. I know who I am. I'm not as good as some people give me credit for being. I believe that whatever gifts I possess were given to me by God, and I deserve no credit for them. My focus needs to remain on building my integrity, not my image.

To keep myself grounded, I ask myself some questions:

Consistency: Am I the same person no matter who I am with?
Choices: Do I make decisions that are best for others even when another choice would benefit me?
Credit: Am I quick to recognize others for their efforts and contributions to my success?

If I can answer yes to these questions, then there's a good chance I'm not getting off track in this area.

Where are you susceptible to character pitfalls? What values do you hold dear? What decisions do you need to make before you face temptation? What questions do you need to continually ask yourself to manage yourself? These are some of the most important things you can think about as a leader, because if you can keep yourself on the road and from going off the cliff, you can continue to lead others and make a difference.

Humility

Nobody likes working with a leader who is full of himself and works only for his own benefit. People want to work with a leader who displays humility. What does it mean to be humble? I like what Robert

F. Morneau wrote in *Humility: 31 Reflections on Christian Virtues.* He said of humility, "It is that habitual quality whereby we live in the truth of things: the truth that we are creatures and not the Creator; the truth that our life is a composite of good and evil, light and darkness; the truth that in our littleness we have been given extravagant dignity. . . . Humility is saying a radical 'yes' to the human condition."[11]

I love that. Yes, we are flawed. Yes, we make mistakes. Yes, we are human. That's okay.

Dale Carnegie said, "If you tell me how you get your feeling of importance, I'll tell you what you are." Where and how we seek validation impacts character. As a young man, I wanted to make a big splash. That's what was important to me. In the beginning it was all about me, my goals, and my success. Slowly I realized that I was not on earth to see how important I could become but to see how much of a difference I could make in the lives of others.

> Humility is saying a radical "yes" to the human condition.
>
> —ROBERT F. MORNEAU

Artist John Ruskin asserted, "I believe that the first test of a truly great man is his humility. I don't mean by humility, doubt of his power. But really great men have a curious feeling that the greatness is not of them, but through them." For most people, humility has to be earned. It is developed over time as you accept your weaknesses and give grace to others for theirs.

In college I read these words written by Thomas à Kempis: "Be not angry that you cannot make others as you wish them to be, since you cannot make yourself as you wish to be." That made a strong impression on me because at the time I did want to change others. I had to learn how to focus on changing and improving myself. That happens only when you acknowledge that your flaws are great enough that they need to be addressed. That requires—and creates—humility. And when you begin to develop humility, you are in a better position to serve the people you lead.

Courage

Courage makes character possible. It empowers us to do what's right in the face of fear, fatigue, or uncertainty. Character is not developed in ease and quiet. Only through experience and trial and suffering can the soul be strengthened.

> Be not angry that you cannot make others as you wish them to be, since you cannot make yourself as you wish to be.
>
> —THOMAS À KEMPIS

There are times in every leader's life when he feels obligated to take people where he himself has not yet gone, to talk farther than he has walked. I know that has been true for me. At such times I do not feel competent enough, experienced enough, strong enough, faithful enough, wise enough, or qualified enough. At those times I must acknowledge my weaknesses, ask for God and others to help me, and summon the courage to take action.

Continuing to live a life of character requires ongoing reflection, brutal honesty, and courage to do the right thing. And sometimes we have to work to restore good character after making bad decisions. That takes time, intentionality, and effort.

Recently one of my John Maxwell Team coaches sent me a poem about leadership and character after attending one of our training events. I think it captures the courage required to develop and maintain character.

The Mirror and Me

When I look in the mirror, what do I see?
Reflections of a double-sided me.
One side is everything I ever hope to be.
Yet my greatest problem is staring back at me.
There are times when I rush out to get ahead,
And I find myself leading when I need to be led.
Courage is needed—how can I overcome me?
How can I lead others with authenticity?

I will remember the best and worst in me.
Doing this will keep me growing humbly.
I will seek others out more faithful than me,
And ask for help with my vulnerabilities.
To lead and do right, that is my possibility.
To do this, I will visit my mirror regularly.

If you want to develop the kind of character that will sustain you as a leader, then embrace the four dimensions to character: authenticity, self-management, humility, and courage. And never be afraid to admit you are wrong. Doing so is like saying you are wiser today than you were yesterday.

3. Character Makes You Bigger on the Inside Than on the Outside

Plutarch, an ancient Greek philosopher, said, "What we achieve inwardly will change outer reality." That has always been true. Character is built on the inside before it shows up on the outside.

The difference between our inner and outer selves is described by *New York Times* columnist David Brooks. Based on a book that influenced him, *Lonely Man of Faith* by Rabbi Joseph Soloveitchik, Brooks said that people feel the pull of their internal and external selves, which are a reflection of Adam from the Old Testament. In Genesis, the creation of Adam is described twice, and these two descriptions characterize the divided nature within all of us. Brooks called them Adam I and Adam II.

Adam I wants to build, create, produce, and discover things. He wants to have high status and win victories. Adam II is the internal Adam. Adam II wants to embody certain moral qualities. Adam II wants to have a serene inner character, a quiet but solid sense of right and wrong—not only to do good, but to be good. Adam II wants to love intimately, to sacrifice self in the service of others, to live in obedience to some transcendent truth, to have a cohesive inner soul that honors creation and one's own possibilities.[12]

The world cheers for the Adam I in all of us. But I believe when we focus on developing Adam II, we choose the kind of character that is able to sustain us, and that is able to fuel and give wisdom to the first Adam in all of us. As Brooks said of that inner character,

> [It] lives by an inverse logic. It's moral logic, not an economic one. You have to give to receive. You have to surrender to something outside yourself to gain strength within yourself. You have to conquer your desire to get what you crave. Success leads to the greatest failure, which is pride. Failure leads to the greatest success, which is humility and learning. In order to fulfill yourself, you have to forget yourself. In order to find yourself, you have to lose yourself.[13]

The inner voice wants to make you bigger on the inside. The outer voice wants to make you bigger on the outside. The voice you listen to wins the battle. When your inner voice says, *I have done wrong*, you have a chance to deal with the feelings of character incongruence or hypocrisy by making changes. That allows you to regain your character equilibrium.

> Success leads to the greatest failure, which is pride. Failure leads to the greatest success, which is humility and learning.
>
> —DAVID BROOKS

The outer voice encourages you to *appear* bigger on the outside, often at the expense of who you are on the inside. It creates a cognitive dissonance, an unhealthy hypocrisy. That outer voice might say something like, "What I say and what I do are not the same and never will be. That's the way it is. Just keep up appearances." That's not a good road for anyone to go down. It's especially bad for leaders, because they can become inauthentic, rationalizing, and unteachable.

I deal with this tension all the time. I know that what I say and what I do are not always in alignment, but I am working on becoming more consistent. I'm not there yet, but I am getting there. I don't give heed to the outer voice, which encourages image. I try to listen to the inner voice, which encourages integrity.

To develop character and become bigger on the inside than the outside, I must deal with my weaknesses. I must embrace failure and learn from it. I must choose the better path forward. For years I had an accountability partner who each month would ask me five questions that dealt with my character. The last question he always asked was, "Have you lied to any of the four previous questions?" Often I would have to say yes, we would have to go back, and I would have to confess my fault. That last question was designed to keep me from developing a divided life.

Activist and founder of the Center for Courage and Renewal Parker J. Palmer described what happens when we allow ourselves to become divided:

> I pay a steep price when I live a divided life—feeling fraudulent, anxious about being found out, and depressed by the fact that I am denying my own selfhood. The people around me pay a price as well, for now they walk on ground made unstable by my dividedness. How can I affirm another's identity when I deny my own? How can I trust another's integrity when I defy my own? A fault line runs down the middle of my life, and whenever it cracks open—divorcing my words and actions from the truth I hold within—things around me get shaky and start to fall apart.[14]

The result of developing strong character on the inside is self-respect, which comes, not from accomplishments or achievements, but from making the right choices. Brooks wrote, "It is earned by being better than you used to be, by being dependable in times of testing, straight in times of temptation. It emerges in one who is morally dependable. Self-respect is produced by inner triumphs, not external ones."[15]

By focusing on internal character, we also care for our souls. John Ortberg offered some keen insight into this in his book *Soul Keeping*:

> Self-respect is produced by inner triumphs, not external ones.
>
> —DAVID BROOKS

Your soul is what integrates your will (your intentions), your mind (your thoughts and feelings, your values and conscience), and your body (your face, body language, and actions) into a single life. A soul is healthy—well-ordered—when there is harmony between these three entities and God's intent for all creation. When you're connected with God and other people in life, you have a healthy soul.[16]

Ortberg went on to explain, "Our world has replaced the word *soul* with the word *self*, and they are not the same thing. The more we focus on our selves, the more we neglect our souls."[17]

A healthy soul is whole. It's not fractured. It has internal integrity. *Integrity* means more than following a moral code. Integrity is defined as "the quality or the state of being complete; unbroken condition; wholeness; entirety."[18] Its Latin root is the same as the word *integer*, a whole number. It's the opposite of being divided. A divided life separates us from our soul. A life that's whole strengthens our character, making us bigger on the inside.

When our souls lose that wholeness on the inside, we struggle on the outside. As Ortberg said, referring to an experience trying to ride a mechanical bull, "If your soul lacks a center when life comes at you fast, you will be thrown off the bull. No matter how hard you try to hold on, eventually you'll get thrown. The soul without a center finds its identity in externals."[19]

Where do you look to establish your identity? At your image, your accomplishments, your recognition? Or do you get it from your internal character? Do you focus on making right choices, on improving yourself, on following through with your commitments, on nurturing the health of your soul? If you focus on the outside, you will neglect the inside. However, if you focus on the inside, the outside will always benefit.

Recently I read an article about Theo Epstein, the president of baseball operations for the Chicago Cubs. People have begun recognizing him because in 2016 the Cubs finally won the World Series, something that hadn't happened since 1908! He had worked for several teams, including the Boston Red Sox, before going to Chicago. But by the time he got there, he'd learned the importance of character.

"I used to scoff at it, when I first took the job in Boston," Epstein said, referring to a focus on character. "I just felt like, *You know how we're going to win? By getting guys who get on base more than the other team, and by getting pitchers who miss bats and get ground balls.* Talent wins. But . . . it's like every year I did the job, I just developed a greater appreciation for how much the human element matters and how much more you can achieve as a team when you have players who care about winning, care about each other, develop those relationships, have those conversations. It creates an environment where the sum is greater than the parts."[20]

Epstein was hired as the Cubs' president in October 2011. In January 2012 he met with all of the organization's managers, coaches, trainers, and operations personnel. They spent one day talking about hitting, one on pitching, one on defense and baserunning, and one on character. Those became the foundation to achieve the one goal Epstein had for the organization: win a world championship.

In his fifth season with a young team, Epstein was on the cusp of achieving that goal. *Sports Illustrated* writer Tom Verducci said the defining moment occurred during a rain delay after the ninth inning of game 7, after the Indians came back to tie the game. The young Cubs team didn't crack. They didn't shrink. They didn't stumble. What did they do? The players called a meeting. Verducci wrote, "The Cubs packed shoulder-to-shoulder for a players-only meeting in a small weight room behind the visiting dugout at Progressive Field." He called it "a strong visual of Epstein's ideals of collaboration and character." In the top of the tenth, the Cubs scored two runs. It was enough to win the game, with a score of 8-7.

The Cubs' character had carried them through when they needed it. And that's what we should all work for, whether we're team members or leaders of the team. Character always counts.

DEVELOPING THE *PERSON OF CHARACTER* WITHIN YOU

So how do you focus on developing character from the inside out? I believe the core of character boils down to three main things: embracing good values, practicing self-leadership, and valuing people.

EMBRACE GOOD VALUES

If you've never thought through your personal values and written them down, then you need to do so. What are your nonnegotiables? What lines will you refuse to cross? What will you stand for?

If you have already gone through this process, then look at what you wrote out previously and verify your list. Has anything changed? Is there anything you would add? Anything you would remove?

PRACTICE SELF-LEADERSHIP

The essence of self-leadership is doing the right thing even when you *don't* want to do it, and not doing the wrong thing even when you *do* want to do it. I call this managing the decision after I've already made it. Let me explain. When you determine your values, you've already decided what you will and won't do. Then when you face a difficult moment, your job is to follow through on the decision you've made.

What must you do to put yourself in better positions to manage your decisions and follow through with them?

VALUE PEOPLE

By placing others first, you take the focus off yourself and therefore have a more difficult time being selfish. That builds your character. Think about something you can do every day to express value to another person, especially to people you don't have an affinity for or don't especially like.

And don't forget: you can receive free bonus materials from me at MaxwellLeader.com.

FOUR

THE ULTIMATE TEST OF LEADERSHIP:
CREATING POSITIVE CHANGE

Several years ago I had the opportunity to play at Augusta National Golf Club as the guest of Lou Holtz. If you're a college football fan, you know about Lou. He's an American icon. In 1988 he coached the Notre Dame Fighting Irish football team to an undefeated season and a national championship. One of my favorite quotes from Lou, which he said the first time I met him over lunch, is "I've coached good players and I've coached bad players. I'm a better coach with good players."

Lou is also known for his dry wit. I spent three unforgettable days with Lou at Augusta. During the day we enjoyed playing golf on one of the world's best courses, and Lou kept us in stitches. Lou was the first off the tee that first day. He teed up his ball, hit it, and immediately started walking toward the hole. *What's he doing?* I thought to myself. I turned to Harvey Mackay, Lou's good friend, who was playing with us, and said, "Lou didn't wait for the rest of us to hit."

"He never does," replied Harvey. "He can't stand still."

It was true. All three days, Lou would hit off the tee and start walking. Needless to say, many times we would yell, "Fore," as our golf balls flew toward Lou. He would just cover the back of his head with his arm and keep on walking. I've never seen anything like it.

If we were playing too slowly for Lou, he would say, "Hey, try to keep up with the group behind you." If one of us was taking too much time lining up a putt, Lou would say, "Putt before I die, will you?"

COACHING CHANGE

I'll never forget those rounds on the golf course, but my favorite times at Augusta were when we were sitting in the cabin late at night and talking to Lou about his college coaching career. From 1969 to 2004 Lou coached at six different universities. None of the teams were winners when he took over. Arkansas had the best record of the six: 5-1. All the others had lost most of their games. Two teams had records of 1-10. What's remarkable is that by his second year of coaching every team, not only did they have a winning record, but every team was invited to play in a college bowl game. That's an amazing accomplishment. Leading a team to that kind of success once or twice is a major feat—but six times?

I listened with interest as our "cabin conversation" centered around making the changes necessary to turn a losing football team into a winning one in such a short time.

Lou Holtz is a leader who understands how to create positive change. He's what I like to call a *U-turn leader*, a person who is able to take an organization that is heading downward, stop the negative momentum, change the direction it's heading, and turn it upward, creating positive momentum. George Kelly, a career coach who worked with Holtz at Notre Dame, said Lou had three qualities all great coaches possess: he didn't take anything for granted, he was an excellent teacher, and he was superbly organized.[1] On top of that, Lou is a positive visionary. He changed the cultures of the teams he led. That created his teams' success.

Being able to turn an organization around by being a positive change agent is the true test of a great leader. Nearly anyone can get out in front of people who are already going in the right direction and encourage them to keep going. Very few can make the changes necessary to turn around a group of people who are headed the wrong direction.

LEADING CHANGE CAN BE DIFFICULT

Any person who has led change knows it's challenging. But I believe that people do not naturally resist change; they resist *being* changed. Recently I saw a two-frame cartoon in which the leader asks, "Who wants change?" and every hand is raised. But in the second frame, when he asks, "Who wants to change?" not one hand is raised. That pretty much characterizes human nature. We want the benefits of positive change without the pain of making any changes ourselves. Why is that? I believe there are several reasons:

1. People Feel Awkward and Self-Conscious Doing Something New

Change is awkward—just ask your hands. Don't believe me? Try this: clasp your hands together palm to palm with your fingers interlaced. Which thumb is on top? Everybody naturally favors putting one thumb over the other and alternating their other fingers accordingly. Is your right thumb on top or your left? Whichever way you clasped your hands feels natural. You'll naturally do it that same way every time.

> People do not naturally resist change; they resist *being* changed.

Now switch them. Unclasp your hands and interlace your fingers again, but this time, put the *other* thumb on top. How does that feel? Awkward, I bet. If you're like most people, you'll feel a strong impulse to switch them back to your regular way.

I had a similar problem with my golf game. When I graduated from high school, I received a set of golf clubs as a gift. I welcomed the opportunity to try out a new sport, so I just started playing golf without any kind of coaching. I was a reasonably good athlete, so I was able to get out on the course and play. But I never could improve my game, no matter what I tried. When I finally took golf lessons from a pro, he told me my self-taught grip and swing were the things holding me back. His solution was to ask me to change *everything*.

Boy, did that feel awkward. I knew I needed to make the changes, but none of them felt right. Over the next few months, anytime I was under pressure to make a good shot, I found myself returning to the security of my old grip, because I felt more comfortable with my old way of playing, even though the new way afforded me the opportunity for great improvement. Over time I became comfortable with the change, but it took awhile.

Most people are more comfortable with old problems than new solutions, because the new represents the unknown. Author and speaker Marilyn Ferguson put it this way: "It's not so much that we are afraid of change or so in love with the old ways, but it's that place in between that we fear. . . . It's like being between trapezes. It's Linus when his blanket is in the dryer. There's nothing to hold on to."

2. People Initially Focus on What They Will Have to Give Up

When people hear that change is coming, the first thing they do is ask, "How is this going to affect me?" Why? Because they are worried that they will have to give up something. Sometimes that question makes a lot of sense, such as when you're in danger of losing your job or your home. But most of the time, life is a series of trades anyway. Poet Ralph Waldo Emerson said, "For everything you gain, you lose something." So it's unrealistic to expect not to give up *anything*. However, many people are holding on so tightly to what they have that they are willing to forgo gaining anything—even progress. As leaders, we need to help people overcome this attitude.

I think personality type and life experience impact people's attitudes in this area. For example, some people are savers while others are throwers. I'm a thrower. As soon as I think I don't need something, I toss it in the trash. I don't think there's been a day in my adult life that I haven't had to dig around in the trash can for a piece of paper I threw away before I was actually done with it. Throwing things away gives me great joy. It's just one of my quirks.

> For everything you gain, you lose something.
>
> —RALPH WALDO EMERSON

Most people are more like my wife, Margaret. She's a saver. If she thinks we might use something in the future, she sees no reason to get rid of it. I'll say this: she's not a hoarder. And she's very organized, so our home isn't cluttered. But if I had my way, our motto would be "If we buy something new today, give something else away."

Not only do we want to hold on to things, we also tend to hold on to ideas and ways of doing things. Authors Eric Harvey and Steve Ventura have written about this human tendency:

> The fact is, we all carry a certain amount of counterproductive cerebral baggage that weighs us down . . . and holds us back.
>
> Our loads include everything from once valid beliefs and practices that have outlived their usefulness and applicability—to misinformation and misconceptions that we've accepted (and even embraced) without much examination or thought.
>
> Why care about "baggage"? Because it negatively impacts us, the people we work with, the environment we work in, and the results we get. Simply stated, whatever we accept and believe determines how we behave . . . and how we behave determines what we achieve (or don't achieve).[2]

Their solution? "Our brains are like closets," they say. "Over time they are filled with things we no longer use—things that don't fit. Every once in a while they need to be cleaned out."[3]

Peter Drucker, who has been called the founder of modern management, said that he believed businesses needed to put every product and process they have on trial for their lives every three years. Otherwise, he believed, the competition would pass the business by. Bill Gates had a similar perspective. He recognized that the products Microsoft made would become obsolete in three years. "The only question," said Gates, "is whether we will make it obsolete or someone else will." I'd say he understands the price of change and is willing to pay it as a leader.

3. PEOPLE ARE AFRAID OF BEING RIDICULED

People who do something different always run the risk of being mocked or ridiculed, and that can be a great deterrent to change. Author

Malcolm Gladwell recently did a podcast on this subject that looked at Hall of Fame basketball player Wilt Chamberlain. It was called "The Big Man Can't Shoot."[4]

Chamberlain, who played professionally from 1959 to 1973, was a dominating center who set multiple NBA records. But he was also known for being a notoriously bad free throw shooter. His career average was 51 percent.[5] But in the 1961–62 season, Chamberlain tried changing something in his game to improve his free throws. Instead of doing the traditional overhead shot that nearly all basketball players currently use, Chamberlain tried using the style employed by Rick Barry, who at that time was the game's best free throw shooter. Chamberlain used the "granny shot," where he held the ball between his legs and shot it underhand.

Rick Barry's career free throw percentage was over 89 percent.[6] In the podcast with Gladwell, Barry explained why he decided to use that motion to shoot free throws his entire career:

> From the physics standpoint, it's a much better way to shoot. Less things that can go wrong, less things that you have to worry about repeating properly in order for it to be successful. But the other thing is . . . who walks around like this [raising his hand up in front of him]? This is not a natural position. When I shoot underhand in free throws, where are my arms? Hanging straight down, the way they are normally. And so I'm totally and completely relaxed. It's not in the situation where I have to worry about my muscles getting tense or tight. And then the shot itself, it's a much softer shot. So many of my shots, even if they're a little off, they hit so nice and soft, and they'll still fall in the basket.[7]

While experimenting with Barry's underhand shooting method for free throws, on March 2, 1962, Chamberlain did something no one had ever done before and no one has ever done since: he scored 100 points in an NBA game. That night, 28 of those points came from free throws. He made 28 of 30 from the line.

Despite his success, Chamberlain gave up the "granny shot" and went back to his old way of shooting—and his old habit of missing. Why?

He was embarrassed by it. Gladwell quotes what Chamberlain wrote in his autobiography: "I felt silly, like a sissy, shooting underhanded. I know I was wrong. I know some of the best foul shooters in history shot that way. Even now, the best one in the NBA, Rick Barry, shoots underhanded. I just couldn't do it."[8]

Some people are more easily embarrassed than others. While Rick Barry didn't care what people thought of him and shot free throws in a style others mocked, Wilt Chamberlain cared what others thought and didn't want to be ridiculed. As a leader, when you introduce changes, you have to take this kind of fear into account, and you have to be aware that people have different levels of tolerance to ridicule.

4. People Personalize Change and May Feel Alone in the Process

Most of the time when people experience change, particularly in businesses and organizations, they are not alone in the process, but they do often feel that way. And their emotions can overwhelm them. When anxiety rises, motivation falls. As leaders, we can become impatient and want them to get a grip and get over it. Instead, we need to show patience, acknowledge their humanness, and work with them. Not only will this help them process the change, but it will help us to influence them more quickly and move them forward.

I confess that I didn't do this well as a young leader. I would often encourage people to ignore their feelings during times of change. I would tell them, "It's no big deal. We're all in this together. Don't worry about it." But that's like a dentist saying, "This won't hurt a bit." When you hear that, you know he's right. It won't hurt a bit. It will hurt a lot!

As a young leader, I also made the mistake of treating change as if it were an event instead of a process. It took me awhile to realize that people are always at different levels in their readiness to change. You can't just announce a change, implement it, and move on. That only causes resistance. You have to give people time and allow them to process changes. While not everyone will get on board or "catch up," many will if you are willing to help them. Remember: the people are why you do what you do as a leader. How far you can travel isn't the point; it's how far you are able to take your people. That's the purpose of leadership.

> How far you can travel isn't the point; it's how far you are able to take your people.

Leading people through change can be a lot like the old jokes about how many people it takes to a change a light bulb. It can be challenging and humorous. Here are some favorites of those jokes I recently came across:

Q: *How many actors does it take to change a light bulb?*
A: Only one. They don't like to share the spotlight.

Q: *How many academics does it take to change a light bulb?*
A: None. That's what research students are for.

Q: *How many aerobics instructors does it take to change a light bulb?*
A: Five. Four to do it in perfect synchrony and one to stand there going, "To the left, and to the left, and to the left, and to the left, and take it out, and put it down, and pick it up, and put it in, and to the right, and to the right, and to the right, and to the right . . ."

Q: *How many aerospace engineers does it take to change a light bulb?*
A: None. It doesn't take a rocket scientist, you know.

Q: *How many people at an American football game does it take to change a light bulb?*
A: Three. One to change it and two to tip the entire contents of the ice bucket over the coach to congratulate him.

Q: *How many American football players does it take to change a light bulb?*
A: Two. One to screw it in and the other to recover the fumble.

Q: *How many anglers does it take to change a light bulb?*
A: Five, and you should've seen the light bulb! It must have been *this* big! Five of us were barely enough!

Q: How many archaeologists does it take to change a light bulb?
A: Three. One to change it and two to argue about how old the old one is.

Q: How many armies does it take to change a light bulb?
A: At least five. The Germans to start it; the French to give up really easily after only trying for a little while; the Italians to make a start, get nowhere, and then try again from the other side; the Americans to turn up late and finish it off and take all the credit; and the Swiss to pretend nothing out of the ordinary is happening.

Q: How many auto mechanics does it take to change a light bulb?
A: Six. One to force it with a hammer and five to go out for more bulbs.[9]

I think the real question is, how many people does it take to create positive change? The answer is one person who is willing to lead the people involved in making the change through a process and do his best to take everyone with him.

WE OVERESTIMATE THE EVENT AND UNDERESTIMATE THE PROCESS

After about five years of leadership experience, I finally figured out that I couldn't just change something and expect everyone to happily fall in behind me. At age twenty-seven, I was facing the need to introduce a big organizational change—the construction of a new building and the repurposing of the existing one—and I realized that if I was going to succeed as a leader, I would need to develop a process to plan what needed to be changed, communicate it to the people, help them process the changes mentally and emotionally, and put the plan into action.

To do that, I developed something I called PLAN AHEAD. Yes, it's an acrostic. That may seem hokey, but it makes it easy to remember and easy to teach to other leaders. I've used it for almost fifty years, and it has worked! And I believe it will work for you. Here's what the acrostic represents:

Predetermine the change that is needed.

Lay out your steps.

Adjust your priorities.

Notify key people.

Allow time for acceptance.

Head into action.

Expect problems.

Always point to the successes.

Daily review your progress.

And here are the individual steps. I encourage you to use them as you face the ultimate test of leadership: creating positive change.

Predetermine the Change That Is Needed

My friend Rick Warren, the founder of Saddleback Church, said, "The greatest enemy of tomorrow's success is yesterday's success."[10] To be a good leader, you cannot become complacent. You cannot become satisfied with today's success. That means you need to not only welcome change, but champion it. If you don't, your team, department, or organization will be in trouble. You only need to read the first edition of the book *The 100 Best Companies to Work For in America* to know that's true. It was published in 1984. When the second edition was published nine years later, nearly half of the original companies no longer existed.

> The greatest enemy of tomorrow's success is yesterday's success.
>
> —RICK WARREN

Identifying what needs changing in our organizations can be difficult, because we can become so accustomed to the problems that we no longer see them. That's what happened at British Rail in the 1970s. In 1977, the rail company's chairman, Sir Peter Parker, was trying to decide whether to give the organization's advertising business to a huge, established agency or to the smaller, newer Allen Brady and Marsh (ABM). Parker arrived at ABM with other British Rail executives, where they found the agency's lobby to be a grimy mess. The ashtrays were overflowing, half-empty coffee cups were left here and there, and magazines lay on the floor.

The receptionist didn't make the situation any better. One account says she ignored the group while making a personal phone call.[11] Another says she smoked a cigarette while filing her nails and answered, "Dunno" to a question about how long they would have to wait.[12]

After waiting twenty minutes, Parker told the receptionist they were leaving. At that moment, Peter Marsh, the chairman of ABM, stepped into the reception area and said, "You've just seen what the public think of British Rail. Now let's see what we can do to put it right."

As a leader, you carry the responsibility for reviewing what your team does and looking for what needs to be changed. I like this standard for review:

- If you've done something for one year—look at it carefully.
- If you've done it for two years—look at it with suspicion.
- If you've done it for five years—stop looking at it and do something to change it.

The first step is always predetermining what needs to be changed. Once you've recognized that, you can start to look at the second step.

Lay Out Your Steps

As I mentioned, I developed the PLAN AHEAD process in response to a big leadership challenge at my second church, in Lancaster, Ohio. We were running out of space in our current facility, so I could see we needed to make changes. We needed to construct a new building and repurpose the old one. The problem was that the fifteen hundred people loved that facility and didn't want to change it. Furthermore, I needed to raise the money to build from that same group of people. If I didn't lay out my steps carefully, I risked alienating everyone and failing to take them where I knew they needed to go.

I spent a good amount of time thinking through the process and carefully laid out my blueprint for successful change. I decided I needed to ask questions, listen to people's answers, discuss the challenges, and empower key leaders to search for answers to our space problem. I let that run its course for a year. And as I hoped and expected, the other leaders came to the same conclusion I had, and recommended the course of action I also believed was best. But by then they came to the table with evidence to support their conclusion, they had bought into it personally, and they had convinced others to join them.

Was I happy to move so slowly? No, but I knew the task was huge. And as the saying goes, how do you eat an elephant? One bite at a time. That's what we were doing. And each step forward increased our confidence and strengthened my leadership.

Adjust Your Priorities

In the movie *The Curious Case of Benjamin Button*, the main character tells his daughter, "I hope you live the life you are proud of. If you find that you are not, I hope you find the strength to start over again." In other words, he was saying that if we want to change for the better, we need to revise our priorities to be successful.

> I hope you live the life you are proud of. If you find that you are not, I hope you find the strength to start over again.
>
> —*THE CURIOUS CASE OF BENJAMIN BUTTON*

The biggest danger for leaders at this stage of the process is to confuse cosmetic changes for critical ones. Cosmetic changes are easier to make but are not effective because they don't address things that really matter. They occur outside in. Critical changes are made from the inside out, and are always more difficult to facilitate.

Leaders who focus on the wrong things are like Charlie Brown from the *Peanuts* comic strip by Charles Schulz. Charlie tells his friend Linus, "For as long as I've lived, whenever I put on my shoes, I've always put the left one on first. Then suddenly, last week I put the right one on first. Every day this week I've been putting my right shoe on first, and you know what? It hasn't changed my life a bit."

Critical changes make an impact. They also cost you something in time, energy, resources, creativity, goodwill, or influence. If they *don't* cost you, you need to question if real change is occurring. Of course, not changing also costs you. If I had chosen to throw in the towel as we were running out of space in Lancaster, the entire organization would have plateaued, and it would have been the beginning of the end. Instead, as the core leadership team came together, we changed our priorities and prepared for the next steps in the process.

Notify Key People

Good leaders don't share information about changes with everyone in the organization at one time. They don't try to make communication "fair." They make it strategic. As a leader, before you let the masses know what's going on, you need to meet with key people and communicate with them.

Which key people? I identify them by asking myself two questions: "Who needs to get behind this to make it fly? And who actually has to fly it?" The answers to those questions point me to the people who need to know about changes before everyone else does.

I meet first with the people whose influence is needed to make the changes fly, because if they don't buy in, the plan is never going to work. I'll need to work with them to earn their buy-in. Usually these meetings occur one-on-one or in very small groups. I often take an approach that I wrote about in the chapter "Share a Secret with Someone" in my book *25 Ways to Win with People.* By telling them about the change before it's public knowledge, I'm giving them valuable information, making them feel special, and including them on the journey. It's an act of inclusion that most people appreciate. This personal approach also allows for open discussion, honest reactions, questions, and objections.

I think of these connection times as the meetings before the meeting. If these go well, I share the information with the people who care the most: the ones who will carry out the implementation of the plan. After that, I begin to hold other meetings with larger groups throughout the organization.

And if a meeting before the meeting doesn't go well, then I meet with those key individuals again, and keep meeting with them until we can work through their objections and they buy into the change. The key players on the team or in the organization must be willing participants and involved in the process for it to work.

That takes care of the PLAN part of the process. Now let's look at the next part based on the word AHEAD.

ALLOW TIME FOR ACCEPTANCE

People usually take a long time to accept change. And usually that acceptance goes through three phases:

1. It will not work.
2. It will cost too much.
3. I thought it was a good idea all along.

Seriously though, allowing time for acceptance is a challenge leaders face because they often see more and before their people do. And the announcement of change can be confusing, misunderstood, or even chaos-producing on the team or within the organization.

Recently I was reading 8 *Steps to Achieve Your Destiny: Lead Your Life with Purpose* by my friend Sam Chand. In a chapter called "New Perspectives," he wrote about the need for leaders to keep changing, but his observations equally apply to changes a leader implements in an organization. Sam wrote:

> Change is always necessary. We cannot assume that just because something works today, it will continue to work tomorrow. You must either evolve or stagnate.
>
> Most leaders [and nearly all followers] only recognize the need for change after decline has set in; they don't take action until something is broken. This is illustrated by point B on Charles Handy's Sigmoid Curve. At that point, the best they can do is put the brakes on to slow it down, begin some crisis management, and put a spin on it.
>
> When you're ahead of the curve and making changes (point A),

no one may understand what you're doing or why you're doing it. That period between implementing change and others beginning to see what you saw is aptly known as *chaos*.[13]

Good leaders always allow time for acceptance. But when they find that acceptance is slow in coming or the people are experiencing the chaos Sam Chand described, they take additional measures to help people adapt to change. Here are three things you can do in situations such as these.

1. Slow Down

If you plow ahead and don't take into consideration the slow response of your people, they will begin to make negative assumptions about you. They might think:

- You lacked preparation.
- You're hiding the real agenda.
- You're railroading through your agenda.
- You lack concern for what people think and feel.

Any one of these beliefs will diminish your influence. And they all create greater barriers to change. The solution is to slow down and give your people time. Keep encouraging them. Keep answering questions. But don't force the issue.

2. Make Your Communication Clear and Simple

A second thing you can do is work hard to communicate clearly and simply as people process the changes and come around. Academia takes something simple and makes it complicated; a communicator takes something complicated and makes it simple. As a leader who strives to simplify my message, I ask myself some questions to help me communicate more effectively.

- Do I understand what I am going to say?
- Will they understand what I am going to say?
- Will they be able to tell others what I say?
- Will others understand what they say?

Why do I do that? Because people will not accept what they cannot understand. In addition, you want the people who *do* process and accept the change to help others do the same. They can do that only if they can communicate the ideas clearly. By simplifying the message before you deliver it, you give people who buy in something clear and memorable to say to others as they advocate for change.

> Academia takes something simple and makes it complicated; a communicator takes something complicated and makes it simple.

A fantastic example of this can be seen in an initiative by Roberto Goizueta, Coca-Cola's chairman, director, and CEO from 1980 to 1997. During his tenure, he made Coca-Cola the most recognized brand in the world. In his book *212 Leadership*, author Mac Anderson wrote of the Cuban-born Goizueta:

Though English was his third language, his success is primarily attributed to his ability to encapsulate complex ideas and present them in concise, compelling fashion. Roberto was best known for his oft-repeated description of Coke's infinite growth potential:

Each of the six billion people on this planet drinks, on average, sixty-four ounces of fluids daily, of which only two ounces are Coca-Cola.

Coke's employees were blown away by the originality and audacity of the idea when Goizueta first spoke it. Eventually, closing the "sixty-two gap" became a centerpiece of inspiration and motivation within the company.[14]

The idea of closing the sixty-two gap was a clear, simple, and easily repeatable message that could be used to communicate change. And the message didn't weaken in power as it was repeated to others.

3. Build In Time for People to Process Ideas

If you are working with people in a more formal environment, such as board meetings, and you need to give them time to accept change, one of the best ways to do that is to develop a meeting agenda that creates processing time for them. For many years I used the following format with my board of directors:

- **Information Items:** I began with items of interest to the people attending the meeting. Typically, these were positive items that boosted morale and started the meeting off on a high energy level.
- **Study Items:** These were issues we would need to discuss, but not vote on. Introducing such items one or more meetings ahead of the time of decision making allowed everyone to share ideas or ask questions without the pressure of advocating a particular point of view. If a study item involved a major change, I often kept it in this category for several meetings until everyone had time to process through the issues and come to agreement.
- **Action Items:** I put items in this section only if they had been previously listed as study items, we had discussed and processed them thoroughly, and I was certain that everyone was ready to make a positive decision on them.

By the time most leaders have recognized the need for change, analyzed the problems and possible solutions, and strategized the plan to implement it, they are ready for action. But trying to take action before the key people accept the change leads to disaster. My friend Norwood Davis, CFO of the John Maxwell Company, summed it up with a formula that he recently shared with me:

$$E = Q \times A$$

That stands for Effectiveness = Quality × Acceptance. And as Norwood reminded me, if you multiply an idea with a quality value of ten times a zero acceptance rate, its effectiveness will still equal zero. Acceptance is key to getting results as a leader.

HEAD INTO ACTION

Once you have the buy-in of the key players, the change train can finally leave the station and start moving. Of course, that doesn't mean everyone will be on board. To paraphrase an observation by former senator Robert Kennedy: 20 percent of the people are against everything 100 percent of the time.[15] But you can't wait for everyone. If you have the influence and the people who will execute the change, you have enough to get started, and many others will get on board in time.

Often I hear people say, "Vision unites people." I disagree. Vision divides people. It separates the people who will from the ones who won't—and that's a good thing. When you start heading into action, people get "off the fence," and you find out who's who. You never know the level of your people's commitment until you call them to action. You want to enlist the committed people to help you.

> You never know the level of your people's commitment until you call them to action.

How do you know the likelihood that people will join with you? You need to take stock of your personal influence. Every leader has a certain amount of "change" in his or her pocket. By that I mean emotional support in the form of bargaining chips. Every time the leader does something positive, it increases the amount of change he possesses.

Anytime a leader does something that's perceived as negative, it weakens the relationship and costs the leader some of the "change" in his pocket. If a leader keeps doing things that weaken the relationship, it's possible for him to become bankrupt with his people.

Always remember: It takes "change" to make change. The more "change" you have in your pocket, the more changes you can make in the lives of the people. The less "change," the harder it is to move into action.

EXPECT PROBLEMS

Anytime anyone initiates any kind of movement, problems arise. It's as the old adage says: motion causes friction. Some of those problems come from unforeseen difficulties. Others come from people and their objections. People inevitably exaggerate about the joys of the past, saying it was so much better back then—even if it wasn't. They complain about the pain of the present, as if life were supposed to be conflict-free—it's not. And they fixate on their fears for the future—even the future isn't promised to us. But these reactions are perfectly natural.

I used to make the mistake of taking personally people's resistance to changing or pushing toward progress. People would push back, and I'd wonder, *Why can't they see it? Why don't they trust me? Can't we just get on with it?* I had to coach myself to remember that it wasn't personal. Besides, leading change is already difficult enough without complicating it with unwanted emotions.

The best solution to solving problems is to be proactive on the front end by anticipating the worst-case scenarios:

- *Think the Worst First:* What possibly can go wrong? Spend time running through every possibility you can think of, and enlist other leaders to help you be prepared.
- *Speak to the Worst First:* Let people know that you know how they feel and what they think. And if you discover problems, acknowledge them. Many times people's greatest worry is that they know more than their leaders do and their leaders aren't prepared to work on problems. When you assure people that you know what's happening and you're working on it, you give them a sense of security.
- *Answer the Worst First:* When people start to ask questions and express their worries and concerns, don't avoid the discussion or paint a rosy picture. Give answers.
- *Encourage Them Through the Worst First:* People desire the encouragement of their leaders. If you let people know you're in it together and that you need them, they are likely to want to work with you.

Even the most highly proactive leaders who work to be out ahead of problems still encounter unanticipated difficulties. But if you possess a mind-set in which you *expect* problems and you're proactive, you've done all you can to give the needed changes a chance to succeed.

ALWAYS POINT TO THE SUCCESSES

In their book *Change Is Good . . . You Go First*, Mac Anderson and Tom Feltenstein wrote about the importance of communicating positive reinforcement:

> I'm sure you've heard the three keys to purchasing real estate . . . location, location, location. Well, you'll now hear the three keys to inspiring change . . . *reinforce, reinforce, reinforce*. Many leaders in times of change grossly underestimate the need for continuous reinforcement. *In a perfect world we hear something once, record it in our brain, and never need to hear it again. But in reality, our words are far from perfect.* During a time of change we have doubts, fears, and occasional disappointments. Sometimes there are friends, family, and co-workers reinforcing those doubts saying, "It won't work."[16]

With all the challenges, obstacles, conflict, and naysayers working against people's efforts to implement change, we as leaders need to encourage our people to keep going and keep doing the right things. One of the best ways we can do that is to celebrate their successes, both large and small.

One of my idols, John Wooden, the highly successful coach of the UCLA basketball team, always emphasized the team aspect of the game. Anytime a player received a good pass allowing him to score, Wooden used to encourage the player who received the pass to point to the player who threw it to him to share the credit. It's been said that when one of Wooden's players asked, "Coach, what happens if I point to the player who gave me the assist and he isn't watching?" Coach Wooden replied, "He will always be watching." People desire validation and encouragement. It's human nature.

Positive reinforcement of the successes people experience as they champion change continually validates the changes they make, so point to the good things about the change and point to the people who made them happen.

DAILY REVIEW YOUR PROGRESS

This last step in the PLAN AHEAD process is vital for two reasons. First, it prompts you to make sure you are on track and moving forward. Second, it reminds you to keep communicating the message of change to your people. That's always a challenge because until the change becomes part of the organization's or team's culture, people lose sight of it and go back to their old way of doing things.

Winston Churchill quipped, "To improve is to change, so to be perfect is to have changed often."[17] Certainly we can't achieve perfection, but we can try to get as close as we can, and that means changing daily. As you work to keep the change message of progress alive with your people:

- Talk about the change clearly.
- Talk about the change creatively.
- Talk about the change continually.

If you do that along with your daily review of progress, the change will be lived, experienced, valued, and shared.

THE FINAL WORD IS *CREDIBILITY*

In the end, your ability to create positive change will depend on whether the people you lead buy into you as a leader. The Law of Buy-In from *The 21 Irrefutable Laws of Leadership* states, "People buy into the leader, then the vision."[18] The foundation of that belief is built through integrity, which we talked about in the previous chapter. Often leaders talk to me

> To improve is to change, so to be perfect is to have changed often.
>
> —WINSTON CHURCHILL

about a vision they have for their organization that involves change. They summarize their vision and ask, "Do you think my people will buy into my vision?"

My response is, "Have they bought into you as a leader?" That's the question that must be answered before a leader tries to implement change. Credibility creates authority, and that comes from everything we've talked about up to this point: influence, priorities, and integrity. If your people buy into you, then they will want what you want because they trust you. And they will align with your vision, even if it requires change. That is what enables you to do big things—even turn an organization around like Lou Holtz has.

DEVELOPING THE CHANGE AGENT WITHIN YOU

If you are currently leading a team, department, or organization, there are undoubtedly things you would like to change and improve. Use this chapter's application guide to help you plan the process.

How Much "Change" Do You Have as a Leader?

Before you start the process of planning changes, take some time to figure out where you stand with your people. What is your current level of leadership credibility? How much "change" do you have in your pocket? Have you earned the credibility to make the change you desire? If you have a difficult time making that judgment, ask the advice of a colleague whose leadership discernment you respect.

Start to PLAN AHEAD Today

Use the plan described in this chapter to prepare for the change you desire to make. Describe what you will need to do at each stage. Then follow the plan as you roll out the change.

Predetermine the change that is needed.

Describe in detail the change needed and why it is necessary.

Lay out your steps.

Write all the steps that will be needed to complete the change. Start by stating where you are now, and outline the logical process, step-by-step, needed to get to your ending point. This may take you a significant amount of time.

Adjust your priorities.

What priorities must be changed to align the organization and people to the coming change?

Notify key people.

Who are the key people you must talk to first? Write two lists: the influencers and the implementers.

Allow time for acceptance.

This will be hard to gauge in advance. Plan time for people to process the issues, and then use your eyes, ears, and intuition to judge when people have had enough time to get on board.

Head into action.

Describe what the first steps will look like and how they will impact the team or organization.

Expect problems.

Describe the most likely problems you will face as the change is implemented.

Always point to the successes.

Begin planning ways to give recognition and celebrate milestones as the change occurs.

Daily review your progress.

Describe the method you will use to review the progress of the change. What metrics will you use? Which people will you talk to regularly to assess morale? What specific information will signal that the change has been successfully completed?

FIVE

THE QUICKEST WAY TO GAIN LEADERSHIP:
PROBLEM SOLVING

Many years ago, when I read M. Scott Peck's book *The Road Less Traveled*, it changed my life. The first pages of the book shook me out of my innate desire for life to be easy, for things to always come my way. Peck wrote:

> This is a great truth, one of the greatest truths. It is a great truth because once we truly see this truth, we transcend it. Once we truly know that life is difficult—once we truly understand and accept it—then life is no longer difficult. Because once it has been accepted, the fact that life is difficult no longer matters.
>
> Most do not fully see this truth that life is difficult. Instead they moan more or less incessantly, noisily or subtly, about the enormity of their problems, their burdens, and their difficulties as if life were generally easy, as if life *should* be easy.[1]

It's true that life is hard for everyone. And if life is tough for individuals, its difficulty is multiplied for leaders. Individuals can think *me*, but leaders must think *we*. A leader's life is not his or her own. Thinking *we* means other people are included, and that means their problems are also yours to deal with.

On top of that, in a well-led organization, problems are solved at the lowest level possible. That means that the problems that do rise up to leaders are often the most difficult. They are "too hot to handle," so they land on the leader's desk. There are seldom two consecutive problem-free days in a leader's life. Most leaders are either entering a crisis, in the middle of a crisis, or just resolving one. Maybe that's why when asked, "What is life?" a group of psychiatrists at a convention answered, "Life is stress, and you'd better like it."

This chapter is my positive take on solving the problems that make leadership so challenging. My hope is that this simple, practical advice helps you step up and gain credibility in the quickest way as a leader. What does it mean to be pragmatic? As my CEO, Mark Cole, recently reminded me, pragmatism allows a person to take things that others would consider problems or distractions and see them as opportunities.

Problems don't have to be problems unless you allow them to be. Why do I say that? Because they do hold potential benefits, which is why problem solving is the quickest way to gain leadership. Problems introduce us to ourselves; problems introduce us to others; and problems introduce us to opportunities. I want to spend the time in this chapter to help you understand and embrace these principles so that you can become a better problem solver.

> Pragmatism allows a person to take things that others would consider problems or distractions and see them as opportunities.

PROBLEMS INTRODUCE US TO OURSELVES

I've shared some of my early leadership journey, including the three years I spent in my first leadership role where I learned about Position, the lowest level of influence in the 5 Levels of Leadership. Like any other leader, as soon as I stepped into a leadership role, I was confronted with problems. And facing those problems caused me to "meet myself" as a young, developing leader. Here are the six biggest lessons I learned.

1. Our Decisions Are Often Impacted by Our Proximity to the Problem

Years ago I heard that when spacecraft were being developed for the Apollo missions, a rift developed between the scientists and the engineers at NASA. Knowing that weight and space were limited, the scientists insisted that every available ounce of weight should be reserved for scientific equipment that could be used to explore and report on the astronauts' experiences in space. The goal, the scientists proclaimed, should be to design a space vessel that would be free from all defects. That would leave a large proportion of space and weight for scientific equipment.

The engineers argued that perfection was an impossible goal. They contended the only safe assumption was that something *would* go wrong, but they argued that they could not predict with certainty where a malfunction would occur. Their solution was to build in a series of backup systems to compensate for every possible malfunction. Unfortunately, that would reduce the available space for scientific equipment.

Supposedly the conflict was resolved when the astronauts were asked to weigh in with their opinions. They all voted in favor of the backup systems. Not surprising, since they were the ones who would be stranded in space if something went wrong!

As a leader, the more disconnected you are from your people, the more disconnected you may become from the problems. If that happens, you may lose the human touch in your leadership. As a young leader, I began to understand this and determined to stay close to the people I was leading. Instead of staying in my office, I went to where the people were and walked slowly through the crowd. I wanted what affected them to affect me so I would make good decisions.

2. Our Plates as Leaders Will Always Be Filled with Problems

Early in my leadership career, a dairy farmer told me, "John, the hardest thing about milking cows is that they never stay milked." As a leader, I feel that problems are like cows. You're never really done with them. There are days when I feel like the guy who had four out-of-state client calls scheduled at home before breakfast. Every call revealed a problem, and every client he talked to wanted him to get on a plane right away to help them.

He skipped breakfast and rushed out of the house as fast as he could, but when he stepped into the garage, he discovered his car wouldn't start. So he called a taxi. While he was waiting for the taxi, he got another call about yet another problem. When the taxi finally arrived, he dove into the backseat and said, "Let's go!"

The hardest thing about milking cows is that they never stay milked.

"Where do you want me to take you?" asked the driver.

"It doesn't matter," he shouted. "I've got problems everywhere."

Someone said, "If you can smile whenever anything goes wrong, you are either a nitwit or a repairman." I'd say you're a leader in the making. That is the life of a leader. Problems are what you deal with every day. Expecting anything other than that is being unrealistic. So if you're a leader, don't be surprised when problems arise and it's your responsibility to solve them.

3. Pragmatism Serves Us Well as Leaders

As a young leader in my first position, I was bombarded with problems and called to make decisions. Because there were so many things to tackle and I had no staff, I started seeking solutions through trial and error. With every problem I sought to discover what worked and what didn't.

My experimentation with problem solving trained me to be very pragmatic, and my approach enabled me to lead with a patience-persistence mind-set. Because I didn't always know the best answers, I had to be patient to figure them out. The benefit of that patience was that I was beginning to develop wisdom. When I was successful it fueled my persistence, and I kept getting better at problem solving and decision making.[2]

Over the years my approach to problem solving has evolved. I have become aware of my strengths (strategy), limitations (impatience), and emotions (confidence). The result? I have had to let go of my need to *be* right and focus on the greater need to *do* right. And I try to keep in mind something author Jim Collins said: "There is a sense of exhilaration that comes from facing head-on the hard truths and saying, 'We will not give up. We will never capitulate. It might take a long time, but we will find a way to prevail.'"[3]

4. BELIEVING THERE IS ALWAYS AN ANSWER IS AN ASSET

Perhaps the most important problem-solving skill that I have learned and practiced over the years is mental agility. I am always looking for answers, I always believe I can find them, and I'm always convinced that there is more than one solution to any problem.

I've found that when good leaders are in problem-solving mode, it's as if they are looking at and solving two puzzles at the same time. The first puzzle is the immediate problem, the situation that needs to be resolved. They work on that, but at the same time, they also look at the puzzle of the big picture—of their organization, of the industry, of trends. They look at how the small problem relates to the bigger picture and all its complex pieces. The big-picture puzzle may never be completed because it's constantly changing and has too many pieces to count, but good leaders solve the small puzzle, while being informed by the context of the big puzzle. That requires mental agility.

> Perhaps the most important problem-solving skill that I have learned and practiced over the years is mental agility.

Here's how I like to think mental agility works for a leader. When you have it, you are able to

- Move from one puzzle to the other without being distracted.
- Hold a piece of the puzzle in your mind for weeks or longer with the belief that it will fit somewhere at the appropriate time.
- Allow the big picture to influence the small one, and at the same time give priority and respect to the small one.
- Live with the tension of two opposing forces: the precision needed to solve the problem and the fluidity to determine when to take those steps.

To tap into mental agility, you need to believe you can solve problems. In the 1970s, psychologist Martin Fishbein developed the expectancy-value theory of motivation, which says that people's behavior is determined by how highly the goal they have is valued and how strongly they believe they can succeed in achieving it.[4] That means if you believe you can find answers to problems you think are worth solving, you are more motivated to keep working at them. And the more you work at them and succeed, the greater the number of tools you will develop in problem solving. Thus you create a positive cycle of success.

5. Our Actions Can Make Our Problems Increase in Number and Size

So far most of what I've shared about the lessons I learned and self-discoveries I made while solving problems has been positive. But believe me: I made many errors during my trial-and-error process. Sometimes those errors not only failed to solve the problems, but made them worse! My problems always tended to multiply whenever I

- Lost my perspective.
- Gave up on an important personal value.
- Lost my sense of humor.
- Felt sorry for myself.
- Blamed others for my situation.
- Wished for them to go away instead of working for them to go away.

Through these errors I learned that I needed to take responsibility for addressing the problem, take responsibility for my attitude and emotions, and give my best effort to landing a solution that was good for my team and organization.

6. Problems Handled Well Often Make Us Better

And that leads me to the final thing I learned about myself. When I didn't give up and I did the right thing in the face of a problem—even if I had not initially handled it well—the experience made me a better person and a better leader. The bang-ups and hang-ups of life have a way of humbling us. When I was a new leader, I used to think, *I wish life were easier.* But over time, as I continually faced problems—because they weren't going away—I started to experience a shift in my mind-set, and I began to think to myself, *I wish I were better.* I call that the problem promise. When you handle them well, problems promise to make you better.

> The problem promise: when you handle them well, problems promise to make you better.

Years ago I read that many of the significant accomplishments in human history occurred in the face of problems:

> Florence Nightingale, too ill to move from her bed, reorganized the hospitals of England. Semi-paralyzed and under constant menace of apoplexy, Pasteur was tireless in his attack on disease. During the greater part of his life, American historian Francis Parkman suffered so acutely that he could not work for more than five minutes at a time. His eyesight was so wretched that he could scrawl only a few gigantic words on a manuscript, but he contrived to write twenty magnificent volumes of history.[5]

And I know from my studies of the Bible that the Psalms were written in the face of adversity, and most of the letters in the New Testament were written from jail.

When leaders of good character face problems, they rise to the occasion and are often defined by their response. Bury a person in the snows of Valley Forge, and you have a George Washington. Raise him in abject poverty, and you have an Abraham Lincoln. Strike him down with paralysis, and he becomes a Franklin D. Roosevelt. Burn him so severely that the doctors say he will never walk again, and you have a Glenn Cunningham, who set the world record for running a mile in 1934. Oppress them in a society filled with racial discrimination, and they become a Booker T. Washington, a Marian Anderson, a George Washington Carver, and a Martin Luther King Jr. Call him retarded and write him off as uneducable, and you have an Albert Einstein. Problems don't have to break us. They can instead make us.

When we are tempted to avoid problems and responsibilities because they seem too weighty, just remember the youth who asked his mentor, "What's life's heaviest burden?" The response: "Having nothing to carry." What you face helps you to face yourself, and what you are able to carry defines you.

PROBLEMS INTRODUCE US TO OTHERS

I recently asked a friend about the character of an acquaintance of ours whom neither of us knew very well. His reply: "I'm not able to comment on his character. I've never seen him handle adversity." And I thought, *How true*. You can learn a lot about yourself by the way you deal with problems, but you can also find out a lot about other people based on how they react. If you're a leader, that information is critical. People's responses to problems and adversity impact the chemistry of your team and the outcome of their efforts.

PEOPLE WHO MAKE PROBLEMS WORSE

When some people face a problem, they can make it worse. I used to tell my staff that all people in an organization carry with them two "buckets." One is filled with gasoline, the other with water. When they come across the "spark" of a problem, they choose which bucket to use on it. Will they dump gasoline on the spark and create a real fire, or will they throw water on it and put it out?

How do the people around you react to the sparks of life? Are they fire lighters who blow things up, or firefighters who calm things down? Anyone who enjoys throwing gasoline on the fire is a liability to you and the organization.

PEOPLE WHO BECOME PROBLEM MAGNETS

> How do the people around you react to the sparks of life? Are they fire lighters who blow things up, or firefighters who calm things down?

When you have people who focus on problems, collect them, or multiply them, they also tend to attract other problem seekers. It's an example of the Law of Magnetism from *The 21 Irrefutable Laws of*

Leadership: "Who you are is who you attract."[6] Such people often eventually *become* the problem.

If you're someone who sees nothing but problems, guess what you get in life: more problems. If you see nothing but possibilities, guess what: you receive more possibilities.

The first law of holes says, "When you are in one, stop digging." As a leader, can you help someone to stop being a problem magnet? Can you take the shovel away from him and stop him from digging his own grave professionally? The answer is yes, but the person has to *want* to change and may need a lot of support to change the way he thinks.

> The first law of holes says, "When you are in one, stop digging."

People Who Give Up in the Face of Problems

Many years ago, I hired a new executive assistant. Her name was Barbara Brumagin. She had been my assistant only a few weeks when I asked her to find a phone number for someone I wanted to contact. Within a few minutes, Barbara returned to my office and told me she couldn't find the number. She had given up in the face of a problem.

I sensed that this had the potential to set the tone for our relationship, so I said, "Barbara, bring me your Rolodex." This was in the days before Google and the Internet. "Then come sit down next to me."

I thought for a moment, then started flipping through the phone numbers in the Rolodex until I found a starting point. Then I began making calls. I don't remember how many people I had to call, chasing down the train until I talked to someone who could give me the number, but I think it took me about forty-five minutes.

I wrote the number down and handed it to Barbara so she could put it in the Rolodex.

"There's always a way to solve a problem if you don't give up," I told her. Then I made my call.

Barbara later shared with me that she learned three things that day: First, there is always an answer. Second, the answer is not always easy to find. And third, she was determined to never dump a problem back on my desk; rather, she would deliver the answer. Barbara was willing to change, and that day she went from being a problem spotter to a problem solver. She took responsibility for finding solutions.

People Who Use Problems as Stepping-Stones for Success

In their book titled *Cradles of Eminence,* Victor and Mildred Goertzel wrote about their study of the backgrounds of more than four hundred highly successful men and women who would be recognized as brilliant in their fields. The list included Franklin D. Roosevelt, Helen Keller, Winston Churchill, Albert Schweitzer, Clara Barton, Mahatma Gandhi, Albert Einstein, and Sigmund Freud. The intensive investigation into their early home lives yielded some startling findings:

- Three-fourths of them as children were troubled by poverty, broken homes, or difficult parents who were rejecting, overly possessive, or domineering.
- Seventy-four of the eighty-five writers of fiction or drama surveyed and sixteen of the twenty poets came from homes where they saw tense psychological drama played out between their parents.
- More than one-fourth of the sample suffered physical handicaps, such as blindness, deafness, or other crippling disabilities.[7]

Why did these achievers overcome problems while many others are overwhelmed by theirs? They didn't see their problems as stumbling blocks. They were spurred on by problems and used them as stepping-stones. They understood that problem solving was a choice, not a function of circumstance.

As a leader, you need to pay attention to how your people respond to problems, and you need to help them respond correctly if possible. What does that take? Time, to begin with. You need to observe people up close as they encounter problems to see how they respond. And you need to spend time helping them learn to deal with problems positively. You can't solve problems *for* them. If you do, you'll be forever solving their problems. You must solve problems *with* them—at least until they get the hang of it.

Once they start to see how you approach problems and begin to take a similar approach, ask them to consult with you before they deal with anything major. And ask that they bring three possible solutions with them when they present the problem to you. If all the solutions are bad, ask them to come up with more options. If all the solutions are great, ask them which they would pick and why. If only one of the solutions is good, ask which of the three they would pick and why. If they pick the right one, affirm them. If they pick a wrong one, use it as a teaching moment.

The day before John F. Kennedy was inaugurated as president of the United States, outgoing president Dwight D. Eisenhower shared some wisdom with him. "You'll find no easy problems ever come to the president of the United States," said Eisenhower. "If they are easy to solve, somebody else has solved them."

That may be true at the presidential level, but it's only true in other organizations if employees are encouraged to solve problems at the lowest level possible, and if they have been equipped and empowered to deal with problems and make decisions. If small problems keep getting sent up to you, then you are creating a problem for yourself by not helping your people to be better problem solvers.

PROBLEMS INTRODUCE US TO OPPORTUNITIES

Albert Einstein said, "In the middle of difficulty lies opportunity." Not everyone sees things this way. But any leader who can shift his or her thinking from *Is there an answer?* to *There is always an answer* to *There must be a good answer* has the potential to become not only a fantastic problem solver, but also a change agent for opportunity.

Leadership author and speaker Glenn Llopis has written about the power of this problem-solving perspective. He quoted Karl Popper: "All life is problem solving." Then he went on to say, "The best leaders are the best problem solvers.

> In the middle of difficulty lies opportunity.
>
> —ALBERT EINSTEIN

They have the patience to step back and see the problem at-hand through broadened observation. . . . The most effective leaders approach problems through a lens of opportunity."[8]

So how do you look at problems through the lens of opportunity? I recommend that you begin by doing these eight things:

1. RECOGNIZE A POTENTIAL PROBLEM BEFORE IT BECOMES A REAL PROBLEM

Great leaders are seldom blindsided. Like boxers, they recognize that the punch that knocks them out is usually the one they didn't see coming. For that reason they are always looking for signs and indicators that will give them insight into any potential problems ahead. Every problem is like the one faced by the trespasser at an Indiana farm who saw a sign on a fence post that said, "If you cross this field, you'd better do it in 9.8 seconds. The bull can do it in 10 seconds."

Good leaders anticipate problems so they can position themselves and their team for success. What potential problems do you see in your world, and what is your game plan to fix them when they happen? Downsides rarely have an upside unless you are ready for them on the front end.

2. GET A CLEAR PICTURE OF THE PROBLEM

Have you ever heard the saying "Assumption is the mother of mess ups"? (There are also less polite versions of this.) If assumptions create mess ups in everyday life, they create train wrecks in leadership. The place to start is by getting a clear picture of the problem you face. Financier and business titan J. P. Morgan asserted, "No problem can be solved until it is reduced to some simple form. The changing of a vague difficulty into a specific, concrete form is a very essential element in thinking."

> Downsides rarely have an upside unless you are ready for them on the front end.

That process begins by identifying what constitutes a problem. My friend Bobb Biehl, who has given me wonderful advice over the years, once told me, "A decision is a choice you make between two or more alternatives. A problem is a situation that's counter to your intentions or expectations." So what must you do when you find yourself facing one of these counter-situations? Follow the advice of author Max De Pree, who said, "The first responsibility of a leader is to define reality."[9]

As a natural optimist, I often have a hard time with this. I'm like the guy who went to see the doctor because he was having some trouble. The doctor ordered X-rays, which revealed a serious problem.

"You're going to need surgery," the doctor advised.

"Is it serious?" the man asked.

"It's going to be highly painful and very expensive."

"In that case," the man replied, "couldn't you just touch up the X-rays?"[10]

Failing to see a clear picture of the problem or refusing to face reality doesn't help you solve a problem. My brother Larry, who has been a consistent mentor to me for many years, especially in business and financial decisions, often reminds me of this. After a bad year for one of my companies, I was sharing with Larry how I hoped the next year would be better. With a clearer picture than I possessed at the time, Larry said, "John, hope isn't enough. Face reality, and let your first loss become your last loss."

Larry was exhorting me not to rationalize my situation or justify any bad choices I'd made. You can't solve problems and make progress without having a clear picture of the situation and then taking appropriate steps forward. Otherwise, you risk doing what my friend author Harvey Mackay calls watering the weeds.

3. Ask Questions to Help You Solve Problems

Okay, I have to admit that I love questions. Not only do they help me gather information and seek solutions, but they also enable me to understand what people think and feel before I lead them. I think most leaders are too quick to talk and lead, and too slow to ask questions and listen.

Here is a series of questions I hope will help you to problem-solve and solution-implement.

The Information Question: "Who knows the most about this problem?"

One of the mistakes confident leaders sometimes make is starting to solve problems before they have enough information. They jump to conclusions. Instead, one of the best things you can do as a leader is talk to the people closest to the problem to hear their observations and suggestions. They may already know what needs to be done and only lack the resources and permission to solve the problem.

The Experience Question: "Who knows what I need to know?"

Playwright Ben Jonson said, "He that is taught only by himself has a fool for a mentor." If you are your only source of information and ideas, you're in trouble. Who do you know who can help you, advise you, mentor you? Author Jim Collins calls this "who luck." If you know great people who can help you, you have it. The more who luck you have, the faster you can solve many problems.

The Challenge Question: "Who wants to tackle this problem?"

> He that is taught only by himself has a fool for a mentor.
>
> —BEN JONSON

The tendency when solving problems is to look first at the capacity of people on our team. "Who can do this?" we ask. That's a good question, but a better question is, "Who *wants* to do this?" Dealing with problems requires energy. The person with desire is less likely to get worn down by the problem. Capacity alone is not enough.

The Magnitude Question: "Who needs to buy in, and how long will that take?"

So much of problem solving in leadership is gauging where your people are, what they feel, and whether they are ready to go somewhere with you. As you think about solutions to problems, you need to ask yourself questions: How big an issue is this? How will people's work be impacted? How will it affect their lives?

The larger the impact, the greater the repercussions, and the bigger the decisions, the more buy-in you need people to have. People will buy in more readily when they have had more input into the decision making, even if the solution isn't the one they would have suggested themselves.

The Trust Question: "Have we earned enough trust to make needed changes?"

This is one of the most crucial questions you can ask when preparing to initiate changes. When trust within the team or organization is high, we can make more changes without negative fallout. If trust is low, our leadership is limited and we can make relatively few changes before people resist. That means that even if you have great solutions, you can fail to solve a problem if people haven't bought in. People won't accept change if they don't trust you.

The Personal Question: "What questions do I need to ask myself?"

This final question is a check to make sure you're on track. As a leader, I continually take my own "temperature" as I deal with problems. I ask myself, "What do I feel?" This reveals my emotions. "What do I think?" This stimulates my best thinking. "What do I know?" This draws out my experience. I never want to blindly move forward in problem solving without including personal reflection.

Do you have a process for self-examination and reflection related to problem solving? You don't want to rely on knee-jerk solutions. Good leaders don't just resolve the issue to get it off their plates quickly for the sake of their own comfort. They help create solutions that take their people and their organization forward and put them in a better position than they were in before they experienced the problem. That's what you're shooting for.

4. Create a Framework to Examine Problems and Solutions

Once you know you have a problem and you work to get a clear picture of it, you can start to gather information. But whatever data you collect will help you only if you have a framework for judging what you find out. Otherwise, how will you interpret what you discover?

My framework has six critical keys:

- *Leadership:* How does this problem affect our people?
- *Personnel:* Do we have the right people to help us with this problem?
- *Timing:* Is this the right time for a solution, and do we have enough time for it?
- *Vision:* How does this problem affect where we're trying to go?
- *Priorities:* Are my problems taking me or the team away from our priorities?
- *Values:* Are my values or my team's being compromised by this problem?

Problems can very easily cause us to lose our way or take our "eye off the ball." Often the big picture gets obscured while we deal with the emotion and disruption problems cause. My framework helps me maintain proper perspective. I encourage you to develop a framework of your own to keep from being put off track.

5. Value Shared Problem Solving

The best problem solvers don't work alone. They enlist the aid of other thinkers to help them. And they use the Socratic method of asking questions to gain from other people's thinking. This method helps them become better problem-solving leaders.

> The best problem solvers don't work alone.

I wish I had learned this earlier in my leadership career. I did my problem-solving solo. I only wanted to share the problem with others after I had answers. I was too insecure to ask for help. I spent 90 percent of my time working on the solution alone, then asked for input on the last 10 percent. The reality is that I wanted applause from others more than assistance.

Today my problem-solving method follows a 10/80/10 pattern, where I try to do the first and last 10 percent of the problem solving and have others contribute 80 percent of it. The first 10 percent is often focused on defining the problem for all of us. The next 80 percent of my time and effort is spent on listening to my team's ideas and facilitating their thinking. The last 10 percent is my attempt to add value from my leadership experience. I call this "putting the cherry on top." I can't always improve the solutions my team comes up with, but I try.

Obviously, the key to this approach is having an environment in which people are willing to share their ideas and offer their opinions. If you don't have that, then shared problem solving doesn't work very well. But the good news is that you can foster this kind of environment by doing the following things.

Remove Silos

Glenn Llopis asserts, "Organizational silos are the root cause of most workplace problems and are why many of them never get resolved. Breaking down silos allows a leader to more easily engage their employees to get their hands dirty and solve problems together. It becomes less about corporate politicking and more about finding resolutions and making the organization stronger."[11]

One of my favorite examples of an organization that has fought against silos is the Richards Group, an advertising agency in Dallas, Texas. Stan Richards has built what he calls the Peaceable Kingdom, an organization without tribalism or silos. He even wrote a book with that title. In his organization he prevents tribalism and factionalism by eliminating departments, oversharing information, having people of every job description work side by side in cubes, and tearing down walls—literally. People work in open

> Organizational silos are the root cause of most workplace problems and are why many of them never get resolved.
>
> —GLENN LLOPIS

space. Even Stan's office has neither doors nor walls. And when he wants to update people on company business, within five minutes he can have all six hundred people gathered for what he calls a stairwell meeting, where people on three floors can see one another from the open stairway and adjoining balconies. It's astounding.

If you want people to openly assist in problem solving, you have to get rid of silos. People who want to increase their territory and protect their turf are rarely willing to freely offer ideas that will benefit anyone other than themselves and their team or department.

Create a Speak-Up Environment

When people are asked to share their problems or to offer ideas for the organization, what happens? Do people become silent? Do they withdraw? Do they avoid eye contact and try to keep a low profile? If so, you're not working in a speak-up environment. As a leader, you need to work to change that.

In a speak-up environment, comments are welcomed, participation is encouraged, and good ideas are rewarded. People don't feel as though their jobs are in jeopardy every time they share a problem. And they don't feel as if they will be discounted or disrespected anytime they share a bad idea.

To foster this kind of environment, you need to promote an atmosphere where the best idea wins. If people are encouraged to share any idea, they learn that many ideas lead to good ideas, and many good ideas lead to great ideas. Here are some things to keep in mind as you encourage people to speak up:

- Never promote the belief that you always have the best answers. This will make others dependent on you and less likely to speak up.
- Ask questions. I know I've mentioned this before, but it's one of the most important things you can do. By asking a series of questions, you can help people analyze a problem and think through an entire solution.
- Try to be a coach, not a king. A coach brings out the best in others, helping them reach deep down inside and discover their potential. A king gives commands.

Remember, the best leaders help others see and solve problems without them.

Socialize Ideas

I like what Lennox International's Paul Larkin calls socializing ideas. It's a strategy in which leaders share their ideas informally throughout the normal course of the day to gain acceptance for them before formally implementing them.[12] In this way your people are not blindsided, they have the opportunity to mull over ideas, and they have enough time to improve the ideas. When they do that, buy-in increases dramatically.

6. ALWAYS COME UP WITH MORE THAN ONE SOLUTION

For years I was a very limited problem solver. I would find one answer for a problem, and then I would champion that solution to my people. Today I try to be more creative. I look for many solutions and let the best one champion itself.

Yesterday's Approach	Today's Approach
Settle for the first solution	Pursue multiple solutions
Focus on only the problem	Explore all opportunities
Fear uncertainty	Embrace ambiguity
Conform to the rules	Celebrate the creative
Possess a narrow view	Connect the unconnected
Fear taking risks	Don't fear failing
Have limited choices	Enjoy many options

As you seek to solve problems, list as many solutions to a problem as possible. The more, the better. Keep in mind that seldom is there just one way to solve a problem. The more options the better, because problems continually shift and change. Leaders who don't have backup solutions soon find themselves in trouble.

As you grow as a problem-solving leader, you will begin to see a progression in your thinking that might look something like this:

There is no answer.

There could be an answer.

I have an idea.

There is an answer.

There could be more answers.

I have more ideas.

There are more answers.

There are better ideas.

The truth is that big ideas don't appear—they evolve. But that only happens when you are determined to explore ideas and look for more and better solutions.

7. Cultivate a Bias for Action

One of the greatest dangers for a thoughtful person is to spend too much time on problem solving and too little time on solution implementing. Leaders who don't or can't follow through are in danger of thinking, *Ready, aim, aim, aim* . . . but never *fire!*

The solution is to develop a bias for action. Don't think, *Can I?* Instead think, *How can I?* Then start moving forward. The moment you confront *and act* on a problem, you begin to solve it. If great inventors and explorers hadn't taken tangible, deliberate steps forward, would they have made the contributions they're known for? No! Their belief prompted action and their action created results. Ideas evolve as you move, and better solutions come into view as you move forward. Ultimately, you can't *wish* or *wait* your way through difficulties. You must *work* your way through them.

8. Actively Look for Opportunities and Lessons in Every Problem

President John F. Kennedy was once asked how he became a war hero. With his customary dry wit, Kennedy replied, "It was quite easy. Somebody sunk my boat!"[13] That is the essence of seeing opportunity in the midst of a problem. No matter how difficult your circumstances may seem, there is likely a solution that not only resolves the problem, but has the potential to improve your life and your leadership.

This has been true repeatedly in my life. As a young pastor of my first church in Indiana, I looked for some resources that would help me teach my congregation how to best manage their lives. After days of searching bookstores and libraries, I found nothing. That problem forced

> Develop a bias for action. Don't think, *Can I?* Instead think, *How can I?*

me to find a different solution. That's when I decided to develop my own ideas and use them to teach my people. I did, and my solution was successful. That planted the seed that eventually grew in me, prompting me to write my first book. Then another, and another. Today I look back and see more than one hundred books selling more than 28 million copies in more than fifty languages. That's a legacy I never anticipated or thought possible when I was simply trying to solve a problem at age twenty-three.

Another problem that shaped my life came as the result of my leadership after I left that first leadership position. Under my direction, the church had grown to three hundred people. But within six months of my departure, attendance had fallen below a hundred.

For months I racked my brain to figure out what had happened. And then it finally occurred to me: I had trained and equipped no one. As soon as I wasn't present to be the catalyst, everything fell apart.

From the moment of that realization, I decided to make equipping and developing people a priority. I've spent the forty-five years since then dedicated to that task. And that journey came to fruition on June 26, 2015, when I taught leadership to leaders from Kiribati in Fiji for EQUIP, my nonprofit organization. That was the day we completed our training of leaders from every country of the world. In total, six million leaders. And it all started because of my failure in my first leadership position and the lessons I learned from it.

My speaking style also came to be because of a problem I experienced. When I was in my thirties, I threw out my back playing racquetball. For three days I couldn't get out of bed, and the following day I could stand for only a couple of minutes at a time.

The next week I was scheduled to speak at an event in Allentown, Pennsylvania. When the sponsors heard I had been injured, they were worried. But I was determined to keep my commitment. My solution was to ask for a stool to sit on while I spoke. But when I did the event, I was struck by the connection I was able to make with my audience. I realized it was because I was sitting. It was an amazing lesson. I never went back to standing, thanks to my bad back, and my ability to connect with an audience at a high level changed my life.

As a leader, you need to see opportunities differently than most people. They are a chance for you to learn about yourself, your team, and your opportunities. They provide you a way to improve your own life, improve the lives of others, and gain influence. That's why I say that problem solving is the fastest way to gain leadership. I hope this gives you a new perspective and you begin to use challenges and problem solving as assets to your leadership.

DEVELOPING THE *PROBLEM SOLVER* WITHIN YOU

Whether you want to receive an opportunity to lead or you already have leadership responsibilities and desire to make an impact, problem solving affords you unique opportunities as a leader. Grow in this area by answering these three questions:

WHAT DOES THE WAY I HANDLE PROBLEMS SAY ABOUT ME?

How you see problems shapes your attitude and your leadership. Do you see problems as an opportunity to use your leadership for the betterment of your team and organization? Or are they inconveniences that simply ruin your plans and discourage you?

You can change your mind-set when it comes to problems and solving them. Make a list of past problems that have led to lessons or opportunities, similar to the way I described my experiences at the end of the chapter. Then make the decision to look for the potential positives in your problems from this day forward.

How Can I Enlist Others as Problem Solvers?

Starting this week, when you face problems, begin using questions to learn more about the members of your team, gather information, brainstorm ideas, and find multiple solutions to problems. Here are a few questions to help you get started:

- When did the problem begin?
- Where did it begin?
- Who was first to notice it?
- What are several possible causes for it?
- What is the impact of the problem? Who is affected?
- What other possible negative consequences could it have?
- Is this problem part of a bigger problem? If so, how?
- Who has dealt with this kind of problem successfully?
- What are several possible approaches to solving it?
- What kind of time, expertise, and resources will be needed for these solutions?
- Will people buy into these solutions?
- How long will each of these solutions take to implement?
- How might these solutions give us future advantages?
- What lessons can be learned from all of this?

What Future Opportunities Are Presenting Themselves in Current Problems?

Pick one big problem you are currently working on. As you seek solutions, brainstorm as many creative opportunities as possible that could be associated with the problem and solution. Allow these thoughts to shape the problem-solving process, because if you are able to use a problem to actually move your team or organization farther ahead, you will have done one of the most difficult of all leadership tasks: become a change agent.

SIX

THE EXTRA PLUS IN LEADERSHIP:
ATTITUDE

Think of a friend, colleague, family member, or mentor whom you greatly admire. Stop. Don't keep reading. Really think of a name, and write it down.

Now write five things you admire most about this person. I think you'll gain an interesting and important insight by doing it. So please stop and write down what you admire.

Why did I ask you to do this? Because I've found that most of the time, many of the characteristics we admire in others have to do with attitude. We admire and like to be around people who are positive, tenacious, and expectant. People with a good attitude lift us up and inspire us.

When it comes to leadership, attitude becomes even more important. You need to see possibilities when others don't, encourage people when they are feeling defeated, and demonstrate commitment when others want to quit.

Author and pastor Charles Swindoll pointed out how the right attitude is central to success. He said:

> The longer I live, the more I realize the impact of attitude on life. Attitude, to me, is more important than facts. It is more important than the past, than education, than money, than circumstances, than failures, than

successes, than what other people think or say or do. It is more important than appearance, giftedness, or skill. It will make or break a company, a church, or a home. The remarkable thing is that we have a choice every day regarding the attitude we will embrace for that day. We cannot change our past. Nor can we change the fact that people will act in a certain way. We also cannot change the inevitable. The only thing that we can do is play on the one string we have, and that is our attitude. I am convinced that life is 10 percent of what happens to me, and 90 percent how I react to it. And so it is with you . . . we are in charge of our attitudes.[1]

A good attitude is an extra plus in life. It makes our lives better. And it also makes our leadership better, because leadership has less to do with position than it does disposition. The attitude or disposition of leaders is important because it influences the thoughts and feelings of the people they lead. Good leaders understand that a positive attitude creates a positive atmosphere, which encourages positive and productive responses from others.

WHATEVER IT TAKES—A LEADER'S ATTITUDE

If you asked me to identify the single most important aspect of a successful leader's attitude, it would be possessing a whatever-it-takes mind-set. The invisible line that separates those who get things done from those who merely dream about them is an attitude of total commitment. Great leaders are sold out to achieving success—in the face of any problem—and are willing to pull out all the stops to help the team win. This whatever-it-takes attitude is common in all great leaders, and serves both the leader and the people well.

> If you asked me to identify the single most important aspect of a successful leader's attitude, it would be possessing a whatever-it-takes mind-set.

This chapter is going to put some muscle in your attitude. To be an effective leader, you don't have to be happy all the time or be a cheerleader. But you do need to model an attitude of positive vision during tough times. A leader's attitude must exemplify resolve, tenacity, focus, determination, and commitment. It must demonstrate consistency, see possibilities, and fight for victories during tough times.

This kind of attitude isn't hard to understand, but it can be hard to live, so I want to give you some steps you can take to develop it and embody it as a leader.

1. Disown Your Helplessness

Whatever-it-takes leaders aggressively pursue solutions. You never hear them say, "There's nothing we can do about it." Those are the words of someone with a victim's mind-set. Professor and expert on organizational behavior Robert E. Quinn wrote:

> A victim is a person who suffers a loss because of the actions of others. A victim tends to believe that salvation comes only from the action of others. They have little choice but to whine and wait until something good happens. Living with someone who chooses to play the victim role is draining; working in an organization where many people have chosen the victim role is absolutely depressing. Like a disease, the condition tends to spread.[2]

Unfortunately, the victim disease has spread throughout America. More and more people have slipped from a can-do attitude to one of helplessness. In John F. Kennedy's inauguration speech, he charged the young people of America to ask not what their country could do for them, but what they could do for their country. Hundreds of thousands rose up and responded to that challenge, becoming part of the Peace Corps, which served people around the world. President Kennedy had a whatever-it-takes mind-set, and his attitude as a leader spread to others.

Today, more than fifty years later, the mind-set in our country has changed from "We can make a difference" to "We can make *no* difference." Quiet determination has evolved into noisy demands. How did this happen? The leadership of our nation slowly began to empower government to meet the needs of the people. Responsibility shifted from each individual person to the government. Leaders stopped challenging the people to *be* the answer to their problems and began positioning themselves as the answer. Now people tend to wait and depend on others for solutions instead of being proactive and self-reliant.

To be successful, leaders need to disown their helplessness and help the people on their teams do the same. They can do that by empowering others. Here's how:

- Never make excuses.
- Create a can-do environment where people are expected to solve their problems.
- Model a whatever-it-takes attitude to your team.
- Provide training that enables team members to succeed.
- Challenge people to take responsibility for their performance.
- Make everyone feel valued and important as part of the team.
- Give solid feedback after team members try to tackle a challenge.
- Celebrate with team members who are succeeding.
- Give people increasing challenges to test their growth and give them wins.

In our current culture, it may seem like a tremendous challenge to inspire people to give up their helplessness and become more proactive. But all it takes is belief in our ability to make a difference. Years ago, I read a story from columnist Nell Mohney about a double-blind experiment conducted in the San Francisco Bay area. The principal of a school called some teachers together and said, "Because you three teachers are the finest in the system and you have the greatest expertise, we're going to give you ninety high-IQ students. We're going to let you move these students through this next year at their own pace and see how much they can learn."

The teachers and students were delighted. Over the next year the teachers and the students thoroughly enjoyed themselves. The teachers loved teaching the brightest students. The students benefited from the close attention and instruction of highly skilled teachers. By the end of the year, the students had achieved 20 to 30 percent more than the other students in the area.

At the end of the experiment, the principal called the teachers back together and said, "I have a confession to make. You did not have ninety of the most intelligently prominent students. They were run-of-the-mill students. We took ninety students at random from the system and gave them to you."

The teachers said, "This means that we are exceptional teachers."

"I have another confession," the principal admitted. "You're not the brightest of the teachers. Your names were the first three names drawn out of a hat."[3]

How could three average teachers accomplish so much with ninety average students? The teachers and students possessed an exceptionally positive and proactive attitude. They didn't feel helpless. They didn't think of themselves as victims. They believed they could succeed, and they did.

2. Take the Bull by the Horns

President Theodore Roosevelt said, "There is nothing brilliant nor outstanding about my record, except perhaps one thing: I do the things that I believe ought to be done . . . and when I make up my mind to do a thing, I act." That's a great description of whatever-it-takes leaders. They are fearless and don't hesitate to take a bull by the horns and wrestle it to the ground. They take action. Effective leaders who want milk don't sit on a stool in the middle of a field and hope that a cow will come find them.

Author Danny Cox said he interviewed a reform school graduate who had become a successful entrepreneur not once but twice. When he asked the man the key to his success,

> There is nothing brilliant nor outstanding about my record, except perhaps one thing: I do the things that I believe ought to be done . . . and when I make up my mind to do a thing, I act.
>
> —THEODORE ROOSEVELT

he said that he asked himself the following questions and *really* listened to his own answers:

- What do I really want?
- What will it cost?
- Am I willing to pay the price?
- When should I start paying the price?[4]

Notice that the last question is designed to prompt action. If a leader doesn't answer the last question and make a commitment to a start date, the first three questions don't really matter. And of course, the best answer to that last question is *now*.

One of the best stories I've ever heard illustrating the difference between people who seize initiative and those who don't occurred on February 14, 1876. That was the day inventor Elisha Gray finally went to the patent office with his idea about a device that had the potential to transmit voice over wires. Gray had been experimenting with ideas for the device for quite some time. But even on that day in February, he wasn't applying for a patent—only for a caveat, which was a document declaring that he *intended* to create the invention and try to patent it.

But at the patent office, he learned that just a few short hours before, another inventor had been there and filed for a patent on a very similar device. That person? Alexander Graham Bell.[5] Gray tried to challenge Bell's claim in court, saying he, not Bell, had come up with the idea first. But the court sided with Bell.

You don't want to find yourself in a position similar to Gray's. To be successful as a leader, you need to possess initiative. W. Clement Stone taught me this. In 1976 I heard him speak in Dayton, Ohio, on procrastination. He told everyone in the audience that for thirty days each morning before getting out of bed, they should repeat out loud, "Do it now," fifty times. And at the end of each day before going to sleep, they should say it fifty times again.

"Do this every morning and every evening for thirty days," he said, "and at the end of a month you will automatically respond positively to any opportunity!" I actually followed his advice. It changed my attitude and eliminated my tendency to procrastinate. I suggest that you try that exercise for thirty days. Then go look for some bulls!

3. ENTER THE "NO WHINING ZONE"

Whatever-it-takes people know how to handle their feelings. They put their attitude in charge of their emotions. We all experience times when we feel bad. Our attitude cannot stop our feelings, but it can keep our feelings from stopping us. After all, what's the use of complaining? It doesn't get us anywhere.

Nobody likes a whiner. Whiners wear people out. There is nothing attractive about someone who complains. That's true for leaders and their teams. When I meet a leader who allows his team members to whine and complain, I wonder why they would have someone like that on their payroll. They can get people to do that for free!

> We all experience times when we feel bad. Our attitude cannot stop our feelings, but it can keep our feelings from stopping us.

What's the best solution to guard against becoming a complainer? Cultivate gratitude. It is by far the most effective antidote to a negative attitude and a complaining spirit. Here are three suggestions for how to do that.

Express Gratitude Independent of Your Feelings

Sometimes my heart is so heavy it weighs me down and inhibits my desire to express gratitude verbally. But unexpressed gratitude is like no gratitude at all. So, in such times, I force my tongue to guide my heart and express gratitude anyway, not because I feel like it, but because it's right. Often my words begin to lift my heart, and I *feel* gratitude that matches what I say.

Express Gratitude for the Small and Ordinary Things

There's a story about the immigrant shopkeeper whose son came to see him one day and complained, "Dad, I don't understand how you run this store. You keep your accounts payable in a cigar box. Your accounts receivable are on a spindle. All your cash is in the register. You never know what your profits are."

"Son," responded his father, "let me tell you something. When I arrived in this country, all I owned were the pants I was wearing. Now your sister is an art teacher. Your brother is a doctor. You're a CPA. Your mother and I own a house and a car and this little store. Add that all up and subtract the pants, and there's your profit."

The more we complain, the less we'll obtain. Or as Michael Angier, founder and chief inspirational officer of SuccessNet, said, "If we learn to appreciate more of what we already have, we'll find ourselves having even more to appreciate."[6] And if you can appreciate the small things, the big things will mean that much more.

Express Gratitude Especially in the Midst of Adversity

Few things test our attitude the way adversity does. I greatly admire people who are able to keep their spirits up when they face difficulties, and I try to emulate them. I read that in 2002, immediately after Charlton Heston revealed that he had Alzheimer's disease, he was in high spirits, flying from Los Angeles to Utah with his close friend Tony Makris, the political consultant.

> If we learn to appreciate more of what we already have, we'll find ourselves having even more to appreciate.
>
> —MICHAEL ANGIER

Makris described their conversation: "He looked at me and said, 'Why so glum, pal—you feel bad for me?'"

"I said, 'Yes.'"

"Don't," replied his friend. "I got to be Charlton Heston for almost eighty years. That's more than fair."[7]

When we are grateful, fear disappears and faith appears. And that gives us strength and motivation to act. Good leaders are never complainers. They're doers. When things go wrong, they start working and rallying people to help them.

4. PUT ON A NEW PAIR OF SHOES

The art of leadership is getting things done with and through other people. As a person develops the leader within, he spends less time on personally producing and more on working with others to help him produce. To be successful at that, you need to be able to see things from their point of view, or as the old saying goes, spend a day in their shoes. I think President Harry Truman was wise when he said, "When we understand the other fellow's viewpoint—understand what he is trying to do—nine out of ten times he is trying to do right."

As a leader, I always try to see things from two perspectives: that of the person I'm working with and my own. I use the other person's perspective to make a connection; then I use mine to give direction. But I am able to see things from another person's point of view only if I am willing to be open to that person. Tim Hansel, teacher and founder of Summit Expedition, described the importance of this in his book *Through the Wilderness of Loneliness*. He wrote:

> It is difficult to receive when your fists are clenched.
> It is impossible to embrace when your arms are crossed.
> It is difficult to see when your eyes are closed.
> It is hard to discover when your mind is made up.
> And a heart that has sealed itself off from giving has unknowingly
>   sealed itself off from the ability to receive love.[8]

I love people, but I still have to make an intentional effort to connect with people. I've always made it a practice to meet and greet people before a speaking engagement, moving from table to table to say hello or simply being on the floor in front of the stage so I can chat with people. I call this walking slowly through the crowd.

Leaders need to connect with people, not just for the sake of building relationships, which is important, but also for the sake of building their organizations. When I meet new people, I try to see their potential for a role in one of my organizations. I'm not only assessing their talent by asking myself, *Can they?* I'm also asking myself, *Will they?* which relates to their perspective and their attitude. That's why I need to try to see things from their point of view. If they can and will, then there's a good chance we can work together.

5. NURTURE YOUR PASSION

Leaders with great attitudes and whatever-it-takes mind-sets usually exude energy and enthusiasm, and those things fuel them to strive for excellence. That's why I believe the best career advice any person can receive is "Find your passion and follow it." That's what I've done for fifty years. Because I'm passionate about what I do, I feel like I've never had to work a day in my life. I've simply done what I love to do.

They say retirement is doing what you love to do anytime you want to do it. If that's true, then I'm retired! Adding value to people through writing, speaking, and investing time in my companies is exactly what I want to do. And since I get to do those things every day, I'm getting to do it when I want to.

> They say retirement is doing what you love to do anytime you want to do it. If that's true, then I'm retired!

Author and pastor Ken Hemphill says, "Vision does not ignite growth, passion does. Passion fuels vision and vision is the focus of passion. Leaders who are passionate about their call create vision." I couldn't agree more.

6. EXCEED EXPECTATIONS

One of my companies, the John Maxwell Team, trains and develops people to become coaches and speakers. So far we've trained sixteen thousand coaches in well over one hundred countries. Twice a year the company hosts what we call the International Maxwell Certification event in Orlando, four intense days of training. One of the things I emphasize to the new coaches each time I speak to them is that I want them to exceed their clients' expectations, to always under-promise and over-deliver. I believe that 75 percent of people fall short when it comes to delivering on expectations, and only about 5 percent of all people exceed them in the service they provide, but the people who comprise that 5 percent make the world go around. They also receive the benefits that come from possessing that attitude and delivering on their promises.

Few things will develop you more as a leader than choosing to exceed expectations. This was a key step in my personal development. I was only twenty-two when I accepted the responsibility of leading my first church. The people were delightful, and as long as I visited the sick, preached on Sundays, and counseled those who asked for it, I was meeting their expectations.

But after a few months of doing these things, I began to feel restless. I wanted to do more. My vision for making a difference was larger than their expectations of me. I possessed a great passion to reach new people. I had big ideas. What was I going to do? After a couple of weeks of wrestling with the issue, I came to this decision: wherever I am, whoever I am with, whatever I am doing, and whenever I have an opportunity, I will set the bar of expectations for myself higher than others do for me.

That commitment has shaped my development as a leader for fifty years. It made me responsible for my own leadership growth. By setting my own bar high, I *had* to grow to reach it. If you're wondering how to do that, consider these things:

- *Giftedness:* I set the bar for myself the highest in my areas of strength because that is where I have the greatest potential to grow and become excellent. In areas of weakness, I ask for help from others.
- *Growth:* As I grow in the areas of my strengths and achieve some level of success, I don't rest on that achievement. I try to build upon it. That means raising the bar for myself again. If I don't do that, I will plateau.
- *Opportunities:* I see any opportunity that uses my strengths as an opportunity to improve by practicing and applying what I've learned. That attitude helps me continue growing and improving.
- *Others' Expectations:* I always ask to find out the expectations of people who desire my services. I can't meet or exceed an expectation I am unaware of. I have built my career by making the meeting of their expectations my *minimum*.

- *My Own Expectations:* Since I use the expectations of others as the ground floor for my own expectations, I am able to build upon them. I put effort into discerning what more I can give that will please them and add the most value. My desire is always to blow them away.

This attitude of exceeding expectations will deliver a high return to you as a leader. As I tell my people, if you deliver on what you promise and meet expectations, you will get paid. If you exceed expectations, you'll get another contract. Everything you give above their expectations is *everything!*

7. Never Be Satisfied

The final attitude characteristic of whatever-it-takes leaders is positive discontent. Good leaders are never satisfied with what is. They see what could be, and they continually seek to achieve it. This is what drives them to get better, to achieve more, and to lead their people to new territory. The future belongs to people who are dedicated to making their world, their teams, and themselves better.

PUTTING A WHATEVER-IT-TAKES ATTITUDE INTO ACTION

Someone I know who is never satisfied with past accomplishments is Paul Martinelli, the president of the John Maxwell Team. I have known few people dedicated to a relentless pursuit of improvement like his. Under his leadership, the company has experienced explosive growth. Yet he is still working hard to do more. Recently when I congratulated him for another very successful year, he smiled and said, "John, we aren't even close to reaching our potential. We are still learning our way through failure." As a leader, Paul has a whatever-it-takes attitude, and that's why he is so successful.

I want to acquaint you with the way Paul puts his whatever-it-takes attitude into action. I believe it will help you develop the leader within you in this area of your life.

1. TEST

While others are crippled by worry, fear, or anxiety, Paul is taking action. He never waits for the "perfect moment" to act. It's the job that is never started that takes the longest to finish. Paul tests his ideas by implementing them and seeing how far away he is from his ideal outcome.

T. Boone Pickens reminded leaders of how important it is to take positive steps forward, to put things into motion. He said:

> It's the job that is never started that takes the longest to finish.

> Sometimes the window of opportunity is open only briefly. Waiting is not a decision, although many people think it is. Be willing to make decisions. That's the most important quality in a good leader. Don't fall victim to what I call the ready-aim-aim-aim-aim syndrome. You must be willing to fire.[9]

To help you be willing to test your ideas with action, I have three suggestions I encourage you to take to heart and put into practice.

Challenge Every Assumption

Good leaders always challenge assumptions. They don't take assumptions for granted because they understand that their first responsibility as a leader is to define reality. They need to be able to see below the surface, know what's really going on, and be able to communicate that reality to their people.

The most important time to challenge assumptions is when you're successful. If your organization's growth rate is high, you may assume that your systems and processes are good. Maybe they're not. Maybe you're leaving a lot of money or opportunity on the table by doing things the way you have been. The only good assumption in your business is that there is a better way to do your business.

Always Ask Questions

How will you know whether your test is successful? How will you go about finding better ways of doing things? The answer is to ask hard questions. You can't allow any fear of hearing negative answers to keep you from asking questions. Hard truths—responded to correctly—help you become better. Ask the following:

- Is there a better way to do what we do?
- What can we learn from others who do what we do?
- Who can help us do better in what we do?
- Are the current numbers the best that we can do?
- Am I growing each year doing what I do?
- How can I become better to help my team become better?

Paul calls questions like these the door to willingness—to try new things, take more risks, change what isn't working, and stretch to be better than we were in the past. I love that.

Benchmark Against Your Potential—Not Your Past

Too often leaders determine a good year based on the last year. But great accomplishments never come from using yesterday as the benchmark. That's an attitude of protecting against losses more than making gains. To make great progress, leaders must benchmark against the future potential of their team or organization, and the opportunities before them. Testing is a way to challenge the status quo and reach for that potential.

2. FAIL

Testing can be a challenging and frightening experience. Why? Because it can lead to failure. However, failure is an essential step in the cycle of success. Paul said, "The willingness to fail is essential for the leader to model and the team to embrace." If we allow the fear of failure to control our attitude and actions, we'll never become the leaders we have the potential to be. And we'll never take our teams or organizations where they have the potential to go, accomplishing all they could accomplish.

Paul worked at coaching people to reach their potential for more than a decade. As a young entrepreneur, he wanted to teach other business leaders what he had learned through trial and error. He's aware that some people have a hard time taking risks. Paul said:

> Most people—leaders included—try everything in their power to avoid failure. And they should. But they should not avoid making the big bets, taking the big risks, or initiating the new efforts that put them and their team in the position to fail so that they can seek the rewards of growth. I think what has led us to some of our greatest achievements has not been my or my team's willingness to do our best. We should always be doing our best. Rather, it's our willingness to do our all. To test every possible opportunity, to test every new innovation, to test every person's ability and potential.

To be successful, you need to be willing to fail. You need to maintain a positive attitude and a strong belief in yourself even when you fall flat. What does that mean? How can you maintain the right attitude?

See Failure as a Constant Companion of Success

Progress always means entering uncharted territory. It means putting yourself out there to be scrutinized and criticized. It means exposing yourself to new pressures and demands. It's only human to wonder if you're up to the challenge. A small, anxious part of you would probably rather not take the risk. That part is what keeps many would-be leaders from taking action and becoming productive and effective.

The price of success is failure. As someone said, rockets blowing up on the launchpad is why we have footprints on the moon, and blown circuits are why the world is illuminated with electricity. If we want success, we need to embrace failure.

Highly creative choreographer Twyla Tharp has pushed the boundaries of her craft for decades. In an interview reported in the *Harvard Business Review*, she said,

> The price of success is failure.

"Sooner or later, all real change involves failure—but not in the sense that many people understand failure. If you do only what you know and do it very, very well, chances are that you won't fail. You'll just stagnate, and your work will get less and less interesting, and that's failure by erosion. True failure is a mark of accomplishment in the sense that something new and different was tried."[10]

The only people who have not failed are those who have not tried. We need to remember that trial and error by definition includes error. We have to get used to it.

See Success as Colorfully Varied, Not "Monochromatic"

What would life be like if everything you tried was successful? I think it would be boring, predictable, and bland. The struggles we experience make the successes we achieve worthwhile. Without the pain, how would we be able to appreciate our progress? We need to welcome the unexpected and be open to a picture of success different from the expected.

> The struggles we experience make the successes we achieve worthwhile. Without the pain, how would we be able to appreciate our progress?

Recently I was reading an article about music written by Allison Eck, who works for the PBS documentary series *NOVA*. In it she wrote about some differences between classical and jazz musicians and how they approach music. I found it especially interesting as she discussed musical notes called *accidentals*. Eck wrote:

In music, "accidentals" are musical pitches—rather, musical glitches— that don't belong to the scale or mode currently in use. A more sensible name for these rogue notes would be "purposefuls," since they're always written into a piece for a precise reason. In classical, jazz, and any other genre, accidentals subvert the listener's expectations . . . on purpose.

The coolest thing about accidentals is that they bust out of musical boundaries in the most unapologetic way. Musicians emphasize these notes; they dramatize their presence, as if to say, "yes, you heard me correctly." Accidentals show us just how trite it is to bicker over categories or labels—no matter what kind of working you're doing, the "accident-on-purpose" is a near-universal phenomenon.[11]

A productive life is colorful, not monochromatic gray, and a person's progress can take on many different forms. Failure to achieve what you intended can often lead to an entirely different kind of success—maybe even to a better version of success than you ever imagined.

Failure is fun when it's overcome! Failure adds color when it gives you "notes" you would not necessarily hear. Success is a story filled with good things, "accidental things," hard things, new things, and learned things. So take Eck's advice: "Be an accidental. Deviate from what's expected, but understand the context in which you're doing so. What's the reason for your accident? How does it relate to everything else in your story, art, or design? Make your mistakes out loud, and on purpose."[12] In other words, be willing to fail.

Have a Game Plan to Get Over Failure

Why do so many people get bogged down by failure? Sarah Rapp, a social impact startup consultant, said, "When it comes to failing, our egos are our own worst enemies. As soon as things start going wrong, our defense mechanisms kick in, tempting us to do what we can to save face." In an article Rapp wrote after interviewing economist Tim Harford, author of *Adapt: Why Success Always Starts with Failure*, she said that failure causes a variety of reactions. The first is denial: "It seems to be the hardest thing in the world to admit we've made a mistake and try to put it right. It requires you to challenge a status quo of your own making," she said. Another is chasing our losses: "We're so anxious not to 'draw a line under a decision we regret' that we end up causing still more damage while trying to erase it. For example, poker players who've just lost some money are primed to make riskier bets than they'd normally take, in a hasty attempt to win the lost money back and 'erase' the mistake."

Rapp suggests trying to become dispassionate about our failures and working not to get too attached to our plans. "The danger is a plan that seduces us into thinking failure is impossible and adaptation is unnecessary," Rapp wrote, "a kind of 'Titanic' plan, unsinkable (until it hits the iceberg)."[13]

I have my own game plan for dealing with failure. It's the same as the one I have for success: the twenty-four-hour rule. I give myself just twenty-four hours to celebrate a success or cry over a failure. After that I move on. As a leader, I can't let yesterday control today. Yesterday ended last night. I need to look forward and prepare for today.

3. LEARN

A friend once gave me the formula for becoming an overnight success. He said:

> You show up every day.
> You work hard.
> You try new things.
> You fail.
> You improve.
> You grow.
> You face countless challenges and rejections.
> You doubt yourself.
> You want to quit.
> But you don't.
> And you do it all over again and again.
> Do this for months, years, or even decades, and you can become an "overnight" success.

One of the most important benefits of having the right attitude as a leader comes after testing and failing. That's when we have the greatest opportunity to learn. As leadership trainer Roland Niednagel commented, "A mistake is only a failure if you don't learn from it." Not all leaders embrace this truth. In my experience, people do one of three things when they fail:

- They resolve not to make a mistake again—that's foolish.
- They allow their mistakes to make cowards of them—that's fatal.

- They develop the security to learn from their mistakes—that's fruitful.

I love Paul's insight on learning at this stage of the process. He sees learning as being informed. But he describes it as *being formed.* Failing and learning from it form us into who we are. Paul says:

> A mistake is only a failure if you don't learn from it.
>
> —ROLAND NIEDNAGEL

The exciting thing is that the learning, if the leader is open to it, truly does "form" them and their team in every meaningful way. We form new thinking patterns. We form new communication styles. We form new relationships. We form new habits. We form new beliefs. We form new mental models. We do, in fact, become inwardly formed in new ways, and those new forms become the new and stronger foundations we can build on and live from. The test-fail-learn process creates the new content for our lives and team, and the content of our lives is always the curriculum of our evolution. We learn both what does work and what does not work; both are necessary and equally valuable to a leader. We learn how to motivate and push our team and how *not* to motivate and push our teams.

I have yet to meet a highly successful leader who wasn't a learner. And the best part is that it doesn't take talent to learn. It doesn't take experience. It takes the right attitude. If we see failure as normal and experience learning from it as positive, we can take risks. We can strike out into uncharted territory. We can face loss. We have the potential to achieve almost anything as leaders. And we can help our people to achieve beyond their wildest expectations for themselves.

4. IMPROVE

What's the greatest value of learning? I believe it comes when we improve. That's where the rubber meets the road. Otherwise, what we learn is only academic.

Success often asks the question, "What am I getting?" Improvement always asks, "What am I becoming?" Improvement through growth is the only guarantee that tomorrow will be better. The profile of someone who improves looks different from that of other people.

Everybody	Not Everybody
Makes mistakes	Corrects them
Hears	Listens
Has problems	Solves them
Falls	Gets back up
Receives lessons from life	Improves from them
Needs to make changes	Does

Social psychologist Heidi Grant Halvorson characterizes the difference between those who desire to improve and those who desire to prove to others that they've got it all together. She wrote:

> People approach any task with one of two mindsets: what I call the "Be-Good" mindset, where your focus is on proving that you have a lot of ability and already know what you're doing, and the "Get-Better" mindset, where your focus is on developing ability. You can think of it as the difference between wanting to prove that you are smart, and wanting to get smarter.
>
> The problem with the Be-Good mindset is that it tends to cause problems when we are faced with something unfamiliar or difficult. We start worrying about making mistakes, because mistakes mean that we lack ability, and this creates a lot of anxiety and frustration. . . .
>
> The Get-Better mindset, on the other hand, is practically bullet-proof. When we think about what we are doing in terms of learning and mastering, accepting that we may make some mistakes along the way, we stay motivated despite the setbacks that might occur.[14]

> Success often asks the question, "What am I getting?" Improvement always asks, "What am I becoming?"

Kouzes and Posner in *The Leadership Challenge* wrote, "Leaders must challenge the process precisely because any system will unconsciously conspire to maintain the status quo and prevent change."[15] If you're leading a group of people, then it's your responsibility to bring an attitude of improvement to the team and to help others embrace it. When individuals experience improvement and it adds value to them in ways they value most, it changes their perspective on what's possible and expands their potential.

I want to say one more thing about improvement here. I believe achieving any measure of success can impair our ability to imagine achieving something better. I used to get so excited after being part of any successful event that I would say, "It doesn't get any better than this!" But the truth is that even when we're highly successful, we need to keep looking for ways to improve.

> Leaders must challenge the process precisely because any system will unconsciously conspire to maintain the status quo and prevent change.
>
> —JAMES M. KOUZES AND BARRY Z. POSNER

I think of this as the "horizon of success" effect. Here's what I mean by that. When we succeed, it becomes hard to see the potential that lies beyond that horizon of success. But we can't let that stop us from continuing to strive forward to improve. We need to keep ourselves from becoming satisfied. The old adage "If it ain't broke, don't fix it" can cripple us when it comes to improving ourselves and those around us.

An example of the need to overcome the horizon of success can be seen in my work on revising this book. Why would I revise a book that has sold more than 2 million copies? In the nonfiction publishing world, that's a grand slam. Because I knew I could make it better. That attitude of striving to get to the next level is invaluable for a leader.

5. REENTER

Once you've tested a new way of doing something, failed, learned, and applied what you've learned, you're ready to reenter the race with your whatever-it-takes attitude strengthened and with new ways to approach challenges and lead others. I've found that when I've gone through this process, my commitment has increased, and that has made me a better leader.

In the mid-1970s, while I was leading my second congregation in Lancaster, Ohio, I faced some challenges that tempted me to quit. But I knew that wasn't the right thing for me to do. I wanted to persevere. So every time I tried something new and failed, I tried to learn from it and apply it to my life so I could improve. But that didn't keep me from becoming discouraged. To fight that, I wrote something to keep myself going. It was inspired by Scottish mountaineer W. H. Murray. I kept those words with me on a laminated card. Here's what the card said:

COMMITMENT IS THE KEY

Until I am committed there is a hesitancy, the chance to draw back. But the moment I definitely commit myself then God moves also and a whole stream of events begin to erupt. All manner of unforeseen incidents, meetings, persons and material assistance that I could have never dreamed would come my way begin to flow toward me . . . the moment I make a commitment.

Later, when I was leading my third church in San Diego, I had cards with the same message printed and laminated so I could give them out to my staff. I wanted them to be inspired to renew their resolve and keep leading at times when they felt discouraged.

I hope this chapter on attitude has inspired you to dedicate yourself to developing a whatever-it-takes attitude so that you experience the extra plus in leadership. That plus will give you an edge, not only in your own thinking, but also in your ability to attract, lead, and inspire others.

If you're like me, you benefit from reading positive words to maintain a positive attitude. I'm always on the lookout for books and quotes that inspire me to keep my head up and encourage the members of my team. Recently I discovered something from Mark Batterson, author of a book called *Chase the Lion*. In it he offers what he calls the Lion Chaser's Manifesto. Mark, like me, is a person of faith, so I hope you won't be offended by his perspective. But even if you skip over his remarks related to God and faith, I believe you will find his words inspiring.

Lion Chaser's Manifesto

Quit living as if the purpose of life is to arrive safely at
    death. Run to the roar.
Set God-sized goals. Pursue God-given passions.
Go after a dream that is destined to fail without divine
    intervention.
Stop pointing out problems. Become part of the solution.
Stop repeating the past. Start creating the future.
Face your fears. Fight for your dreams.
Grab opportunity by the mane and don't let go!
Live like today is the first day and the last day of your life.
Burn sinful bridges. Blaze new trails.
Live for the applause of nail-scarred hands.
Don't let what's wrong with you keep you from worshiping
    what's right with God.
Dare to fail. Dare to be different.
Quit holding out. Quit holding back. Quit running away.
Chase the lion.[16]

Whatever the lion is in your life, I encourage you to adopt a whatever-it-takes attitude and to chase the lion for all you're worth. Even if you never catch it, you'll never regret it.

DEVELOPING THE *POSITIVE BELIEVER* WITHIN YOU

I've observed that people are born with a natural bent when it comes to attitude. My father said very positive things to my siblings and I when we were growing up, and he was a constant encourager, but he admitted to me that he was not born that way. He had to work to become a positive believer in his own ability and that of others.

Born Winner or Loser?

What is your natural bent? Were you born thinking you were a winner or loser? Victor or victim? If you're already positive, great. Keep it up. If you were born seeing the glass half empty, you need to improve your attitude if you want to develop the leader within you. Start the process by keeping a gratitude journal. Every morning, write a list of the things you're grateful for. Don't start your day until you've written down at least one thing. And before you go to sleep at night, add to the morning list all of the things you're grateful for from the day you've just spent. Day after day, keep adding to your gratitude list.

After you've done this every day for a solid month, ask someone who knows you well whether they've seen any change in your attitude.

Fail on Purpose

Take a professional risk this month that you think is likely to fail so that you can use the process outlined in the chapter to improve your attitude. Start by deciding what the "test" will be. Write out that first step here.

1. Test
2. Fail
3. Learn
4. Improve
5. Reenter

Once you've written what the test will be, go do it. If you fail, then write about it under number 2. And then move on to what you learned, how you can improve, and what you must do to reengage as a leader.

If you don't fail, then still complete steps three through five, but then try another test. You won't really benefit from this process until you've failed and had to work through it.

SEVEN

THE HEART OF LEADERSHIP:
SERVING PEOPLE

I spent a total of twenty-six years leading churches as a senior pastor. But when I was a young leader just getting started in my career, my focus wasn't initially on serving people. It was on doing big things and getting ahead. All my training and education assumed a hierarchical approach to leadership. Pastors were educated, ordained, and positioned to sit apart from and "above" their congregations. We were expected to preach messages, give wise counsel, and conduct the ordinances of the church. The models of leadership were all top-down.

But then I went to hear Zig Ziglar speak, and I heard him say, "If you help people get what they want, they will help you get what you want." What he was really talking about was servant leadership, and that idea rocked my world.

CHANGE OF HEART

Zig's comment made me realize something: I was trying to get others to help me, not trying to help them. I realized my attitude toward people wasn't right. And that knowledge started me on a journey that eventually made me realize that the heart of leadership is based on serving others, not myself. It challenged me to invert the "power pyramid," putting others at the top and myself at the bottom.

I started to change my leadership focus to empowering others to do what I was doing. And the real clincher came when I read a passage in the Bible as if for the first time. It said, "So Christ himself gave the apostles, the prophets, the evangelists, the pastors and teachers, to equip his people for works of service, so that the body of Christ may be built up."[1] This made it clear that my responsibility as a pastor was to equip God's people to do His work and build up the church. From that moment I realized I wasn't supposed to get the people to help me build my congregation. I was to serve people and help them build God's church. From that day on, my leadership has always been about serving others, and not about being served by others.

> The heart of leadership is based on serving others, not ourselves.

That was forty-five years ago. My thinking about leadership and my approach to it has continued to be shaped by other people in this area. Robert Greenleaf has been an influence. In 1970 he wrote an essay called "The Servant as Leader," which he later expanded into the book *Servant Leadership*. Greenleaf wrote:

> The servant-leader is servant first. . . . It begins with the natural feeling that one wants to serve, to serve first. Then conscious choice brings one to aspire to lead. . . . The care taken by the servant-first [leader is] to make sure that other people's highest priority needs are being served. The best test, and difficult to administer, is: Do those served grow as persons? Do they, while being served, become healthier, wiser, freer, more autonomous, more likely themselves to become servants? And, what is the effect on the least privileged in society? Will they benefit or at least not be further deprived?[2]

Others books, such as *Leadership Is an Art* by Max De Pree, the former chairman of Herman Miller, and *The Soul of the Firm* by C. William Pollard, chairman emeritus of ServiceMaster, also assisted me on my journey to becoming a servant leader. But the book that made the greatest impression on me was Eugene Habecker's *The Other Side of Leadership*. It convinced me that adding value to others needed to be at the core of my leadership. I've had the privilege of knowing Eugene for more than thirty years. The words in his book are a description of his life. He said, "The true leader serves. Serves people. Serves their best interests, and in so doing will not always be popular, may not impress. But because true leaders are motivated by loving concern rather than a desire for personal glory, they are willing to pay the price."[3]

Inspired by Eugene's life and his book, I made two decisions: first, I would place the concerns of others above my own, and second, I would love people unconditionally. The first was a matter of the will. The second was a change in attitude. And because I'm a person of faith, I adopted the following words from the Bible and took them to heart as the desire of my life:

> Tell those rich in this world's wealth to quit being so full of themselves and so obsessed with money, which is here today and gone tomorrow. Tell them to go after God, who piles on all the riches we could ever manage—to do good, to be rich in helping others, to be extravagantly generous. If they do that, they'll build a treasury that will last, gaining life that is truly life.[4]

As I strive to live this way, I've adopted some guidelines that I try to practice daily to become a better servant leader:

- *I Don't Rely on My Position or Title:* I'm grateful for the accomplishments I've made, but I don't rely on them to help me lead. I work to earn respect every day by delivering on what I promise and by serving others.
- *I Choose to Believe in People and Their Potential:* I care about people because it's the right thing to do. But there are also practical reasons for believing in people. I've found that the more I believe in people's potential and the more I serve them, the more their potential increases. That creates a win for everyone.
- *I Try to See Things from the Perspective of Others:* It's possible to lead and serve others well only when you know their minds and hearts. I intentionally connect with people and try to see from their point of view to serve them better.

- *I Work to Create an Environment of Encouragement:* Few things are better than being on a team of people who desire to serve one another. When leaders are willing to serve people and encourage others to serve, a spirit of cooperation emerges where it's "one for all and all for one." That makes the environment positive and develops a sense of loyalty among team members.
- *I Measure My Success by How Much Value I Add to Others:* When you decide to serve others as a leader, the team's success becomes your success. I remember when I experienced that change in thinking. It felt as though my world immediately expanded. It is true: one is too small a number to achieve greatness. Few things surpass helping your team to win together.

I'm still not where I would like to be when it comes to serving people, but I'm continually striving to get better at it.

THE POWER OF SERVING OTHERS

> When you decide to serve others as a leader, the team's success becomes your success.

My desire to serve people comes out of my faith, but you don't need faith to want to serve others. The attitude, priority, and practice of serving others make good business sense and are accessible to anyone. Organizational consultant S. Chris Edmonds defines servant leadership as "a person's dedication to helping others be their best selves at home, work, and in their community. Anyone can serve—and lead—from any position or role in a family, workplace, or community."[5]

If you look at the words of many highly admired leaders, you can see the theme of serving others in their attitudes toward leadership. Here are a few examples:

- *George Washington:* "Every post is honorable in which a man can serve his country."
- *Benjamin Franklin:* "No one is useless in this world who lightens the burden of it for someone else."

- **Mahatma Gandhi:** "The best way to find yourself is to lose yourself in the service of others."
- **Albert Schweitzer:** "I don't know what your destiny will be, but one thing I do know: the only ones among you who will be really happy are those who have sought and found how to serve."
- **Martin Luther King Jr.:** "Everybody can be great, because everybody can serve."
- **Nelson Mandela:** "I stand here before you not as a prophet, but as a humble servant of you, the people."

All these people have one thing in common; they were transformational in their own lives, and the lives they touched were beautifully changed. Their values transferred to others. Their works of service not only helped others, but became models for others to emulate. As the saying goes, they were concerned with teaching people how to fish, not just giving them a fish. They wanted to encourage autonomy among the people and create prosperity for future generations through lasting change, not cultivate people's dependence based on their service to their leader.

> No one is useless in this world who lightens the burden of it for someone else.
>
> —BENJAMIN FRANKLIN

Ann McGee-Cooper and Duane Trammell have an interesting perspective on this subject. They believe that leaders have been positioned as heroes in organizations and in our culture. Instead, they believe, leaders need to shift from heroes to servants. In an article titled "From Hero-as-Leader to Servant-as-Leader," they wrote, "The true heroes of the new millennium will be servant-leaders, quietly working out of the spotlight to transform our world." How should they do that? They list five things. Servant leaders should listen without judgment, be authentic, build community, share power, and develop people.[6]

QUESTIONS TO HELP YOU SERVE PEOPLE BETTER

It is my great desire for you to develop into a leader who serves others every day. To help you do that, I want to offer you some questions you can ask yourself that will help you.

1. THE ADDING-VALUE QUESTION: "WHAT CAN I DO FOR PEOPLE TO HELP THEM SUCCEED?"

Helen Keller observed, "Alone we can do so little. Together we can do so much." Because servant leaders define others' success as their success, they focus on helping others succeed. One of the best ways to do that is by adding value to people.

As I write these words, there are four calls on my schedule that I will make later today. Two are calls to people I am mentoring. I anticipate that they will be asking me to give them guidance on leadership issues. I will do my very best to help them navigate their challenges effectively.

The other two calls are with leaders of two companies for whom I will soon be speaking. These pre-calls have been planned so that I can discover how I can best serve my hosts when I speak to their people. I do calls like these before every speaking engagement and ask a lot of questions, such as:

- Do you have a theme for the conference?
- What are your expectations of me?
- What things do you want me to say that will help you the most?
- Beyond speaking, is there anything else I can do for you?

My assistant, Linda Eggers, always joins me on these calls and takes detailed notes so we don't miss anything. Only after asking these and other questions and listening to their answers do I share ways I think I will be able to help them. And I always verify with them that I'm on the right track.

Why do I go to all this trouble? My role is simple: to speak and serve. I've observed too many speakers who have only a few canned speeches that they use with every audience, no matter what that audience may need or want. My desire is to serve my host and my audience. I'll develop a speech to fit their specific agenda because I know it's not about me. The question I'm asking at the end of my time with them is, "Did I help you?" I agree with the perspective of Tom Peters, who said, "Organizations exist to serve. Period. Leaders live to serve. Period."

One of the best servant leaders I know is Mark Cole, the CEO of my companies. He is the best "second person" I have ever worked with. When we began our journey together, he asked me how he could best serve me. My answer was simple: "Stay close to me and represent me well to my companies." This request aligns with the *Proximity Principle* that I teach and follow: those closest to the leader find the most opportunities to serve that leader.

> Organizations exist to serve. Period. Leaders live to serve. Period.
>
> —TOM PETERS

Mark usually travels with me so we can continually talk about the companies. But when we are not together physically, we are still close together. Mark makes himself available to me 24/7. So does my assistant, Linda Eggers, who has been with me for more than thirty years. And they both do it with joy. Their agenda is to fulfill my agenda.

As Mark serves me, I also serve him. My answer to the question "What can I do for him to help him succeed?" is to give him my time. I mentor Mark. I make sure he has the resources he needs to do his work. And I actively seek opportunities for him to grow. Currently, I'm helping him work on his public speaking.

2. THE EVERYDAY QUESTION: "WHAT DO PEOPLE NEED FROM ME DAILY THAT THEY MAY NOT WANT TO ASK FOR?"

The best servant leaders anticipate what their people need from them. They are proactive in helping the people they lead. Too many leaders have the attitude, "If they need something, let them ask. My door is always open." Here's a thought: instead of leaving the door open, go out of the door to where your people are and *look for* what they need. Then give it to them *before* they even ask. You can't assume that others have the same desires and expectations you do.

I greatly admire Pope Francis. It was my privilege to meet him and observe his servant leadership in action for a few hours. Recently I read a message he gave to the deacons of the church, in which he said:

How do we become "good and faithful servants" (cf. Mt 25:21)? As a first step, we are asked to be available. A servant daily learns detachment from doing everything his own way and living his life as he would. Each morning he trains himself to be generous with his life and to realize that the rest of the day will not be his own, but given over to others. One who serves cannot hoard his free time; he has to give up the idea of being the master of his day. He knows that his time is not his own, but a gift from God which is then offered back to him. Only in this way will it bear fruit. One who serves is not a slave to his own agenda, but ever ready to deal with the unexpected, ever available to his brothers and sisters and ever open to God's constant surprises. A servant knows how to open the doors of his time and inner space for those around him, including those who knock on those doors at odd hours, even if that entails setting aside something he likes to do or giving up some well-deserved rest. Dear deacons, if you show that you are available to others, your ministry will not be self-serving, but evangelically fruitful.[7]

That's great advice for all leaders, not just faith-based ones. Serving others begins with attitude and then becomes action. If you ask yourself what others need and act on your findings every day, serving others will soon become a habit.

I love a song that was written by my friends the Goads. They are a family of singers who have servants' hearts. When my son Joel was a teenager going through a rough patch, they took him on tour with them as part of their tech crew. It gave him a chance to spread his wings and develop his talents and skills. They also loved him and invested in him.

The song the Goads wrote is called "Follow Me." Here's what it says:

I want to be someone who makes things better.
Someone who helps you reach the very top.

Never holding back, doing more than what is asked,
I am going to give it everything I have got.

Follow me, I am right behind you.
Let me help you lift the load.
Let me make your burdens lighter
As we are heading down this road.

I believe in what you are doing.
Let me help you see it through.
I'll do everything I can to make your dreams come true.
Follow me, I am right behind you.

I will seek to answer problems with solutions.
I will give my strongest effort every day.
In trouble and in trial,
I will go the extra mile.
We will reach the goal no matter what it takes.

Never making excuses.
Putting it all on the line.
Willing to do what others won't.
Doing more than what is expected
Even when it isn't my job.
The goal is more important than the role.[8]

Those lyrics capture the mind-set of people who give what others need, even when they may not be willing to ask. As leaders, that's how we should think.

3. The Improvement Question: "What can I work on that will help me serve people better?"

Servant leadership is all about the person you serve. To grow in effectiveness you must value what is valuable to that person. It is not enough to just "get better." We must get better in the areas that are important to the ones we serve. As a leader, do you possess what your team members need, specifically in the areas that can benefit your people?

More than twenty years ago, Charlie Wetzel came alongside me to help me with my writing load. Charlie could write, but he didn't really know me well. The first thing I did was give him a set of one hundred of my lessons on cassette so that he could start to understand my speaking style. But I knew that wasn't enough. I needed to be proactive in serving him so that he could serve me and my organizations.

One of the things I did was give Charlie a book of quotes and ask him to mark what he considered the best ones. After he did that, I looked through the same book and marked the quotes I thought were the best. Then we compared our choices. In the beginning, 90 percent of our choices didn't match. So I explained why I liked the quotes I picked so that he understood my thinking. Then we did this exercise again, and again. After doing this a few times, our choices matched 90 percent of the time. If I hadn't taken responsibility for trying to help Charlie, it would have made his job much more difficult.

To bring out the best in others, I first have to bring out the best in me. I cannot give what I do not have. Neither can you. And here's the good news: your self-respect will be strengthened as you become better. The wins you experience on the outside with your team will be the result of the victories you first experience on the inside. Each step of improvement will allow you to feel good about yourself and your journey. As my friend Mark Cole says, "A servant leader's value rests in why he does what he does and how well he does it, not in what he does or how often he does it. This allows him to find value in who he is."

> To bring out the best in others, I have to first bring out the best in me. I cannot give what I do not have. Neither can you.

As a servant leader, when you improve yourself in areas that are important to the people you lead, not only do you get better, but you make the person you serve better. That compounds your and their effectiveness. And it has a high return both personally and organizationally.

4. THE EVALUATION QUESTION: "HOW WILL I KNOW THAT I AM SERVING PEOPLE WELL?"

One of the lessons I teach in *The Leadership Handbook* is this: to see how the leader is doing, look at the people. Often the answer to how well the leader is doing is clear to outside observers. But how do the leaders themselves discover the answer? How do they know whether they are serving their people well?

Yesterday I invested an hour in mentoring a young leader who has great potential. One of the things he asked me was "What are the essentials that I need to know and do as I begin to establish my leadership?" My answer was two words: *questions* and *expectations*. My advice to him also helps leaders know how they are serving their people.

It's essential to ask questions as a leader. How else will you know where your people are mentally and emotionally? How else will you know what they want and need? How else will you know how to lead them? As a young leader, I used to give direction and then ask questions. (The questions were mostly to verify that people understood my direction.) Today I ask questions first before I even try to give direction.

Setting expectations is also essential. In my younger years I would try to "sneak" expectations into the dialogue with my team members, giving them a little bit at a time, hoping over time they would get it so that I wouldn't have to be too direct. Too many times they never did understand what I wanted. That frustrated both of us. Today I set up expectations at the beginning of any endeavor. This gives clarity to the entire team. I also ask to know the expectations of the people I'm leading. I need to know what a win looks like to them.

I've talked a lot about Mark Cole, my CEO, because he is such a wonderful servant leader. He serves me well and serves the people in the organizations he leads. In fact, he goes above and beyond and always works hard to exceed my expectations. He delivers—and then some.

While I was preparing to write this chapter, I asked Mark, "How is it that you consistently exceed expectations for the team?" His answer was very revealing. He said there are five things he continually does:

- Stay close to me so he can know what I'm thinking; this allows him to communicate my vision to the team.
- Check with me to make certain that he is on track serving the companies.
- Ask himself, "How can I exceed expectations for our clients and the team?"
- Continually ask the team how they believe they can exceed client expectations.
- Take personal responsibility for delivering what others need and then some.

Mark tells me that I have a higher belief in him than he does in himself, which helps to fuel him. I feel that's the least I can do to serve him. And as a leader, I want him to transfer that belief to the people he leads.

If you had to give yourself a report card on how you're serving your people, how would you score yourself? Do you know what your people's expectations are for you, and are you sharing your expectations clearly? Are you asking your people questions so they can tell you what you're doing well and where you could improve? If you're not evaluating your performance in serving them, you're probably not doing it as well as you could be.

5. THE BLIND SPOT QUESTION: "WHAT IS IT LIKE FOR THE PEOPLE WHO WORK WITH ME?"

This question is my favorite because it has helped me the most. We all have blind spots, things we don't see about ourselves. I don't always see myself as others see me, and I don't always see things as others do. I'm certain those things are also true for you.

If you have leadership responsibilities, your blind spots are compounded. Because leaders have power and authority, the people around them are often intimidated and think they cannot be open and honest with them. And the higher you are in leadership, the more difficult it is to get a true read on what's happening around you. People often tell leaders what they want to hear, not what they need to hear. So that means as a leader, you have personal blind spots *plus* you don't always receive honest feedback from the people who know your faults.

How can this challenge be overcome? As a leader, I make two assumptions. First, I assume I have blind spots that hurt me. Second, I recognize that others could be intimidated and may not always be willing to help me with them. Therefore, I ask this question, "What is it like to be on the other side of the table from me?"

The answers I discover are not always comfortable, but if I maintain a good attitude, they can help me to be self-correcting. Here are some examples of what I know about myself:

- I always think things can be done more quickly than they actually can.
- I don't appreciate the struggles most people deal with.
- I too often assume people instantly understand my vision and will line up with it.
- I'm impatient. (That's short and to the point.)
- I believe everyone is capable of doing what I do if they are willing to put in the effort.
- I move on from difficulties quickly and expect others to do the same at my speed.

I could go on and on, but I don't want to bore you. You get the idea.

To try to overcome my many blind spots, I am always asking, "What am I missing?" and "Can you help me?" I have given the people around me permission to speak truth into my life. It is the only way I can be protected from my blind spots.

Another question I continually ask myself is "Am I working to serve the people around me or for my own personal gain?" The honest answer should be both. However, if my own personal gain continually outweighs serving others, there is a problem with my leadership. I've lost the heart of leading others, and I have to remind myself that if I put serving others first, then personal gain will usually come on the heels of it automatically.

Recently I read some great advice that helps me stay grounded as a servant leader. It came from Dan Price, the founder and CEO of Gravity Payments, a credit card–processing company that supports independent business. Price wrote that to become servant leaders, people should do the following:

1. Instead of spending your time defining expectations for your team, spend it identifying how you can support them.
2. Have your team keep an eye on your actions rather than the other way around.
3. Ask for feedback rather than telling your team what to do.
4. Resist the urge to accumulate power. Focus on giving it away.[9]

What is it like for people who sit on the other side of the table or desk from you? Have you thought about that? Too often we assume it's easy. Often it's not. The stronger your leadership and your personality, the more difficult it is for others to work with you. Cultivate a servant's heart and you help to diminish that difficulty for the people you lead.

6. THE RESPECT QUESTION: "HOW CAN I GAIN VALUE WHILE ADDING VALUE TO OTHERS BY SERVING?"

Many years ago, I read *Bringing Out the Best in People* by Alan Loy McGinnis. It was a book that I would read and reread because I found the message so impacting. The statement that made the greatest lasting impression on me was "There is no more noble occupation in the world than to assist another human being, to help someone else succeed."[10]

> There is no more noble occupation in the world than to assist another human being, to help someone else succeed.
>
> —ALAN LOY MCGINNIS

In 1995 when I resigned my prestigious position as the senior pastor of Skyline Church, I did so because I was making an intentional transition. I had developed leaders in my congregations for twenty years, but I had started to wonder what would happen if I spent *all* of my time serving leaders all over the country.

What if I spent my time helping others reach new levels of success instead of just being successful myself?

I made the change and didn't look back. Now, more than twenty years later, I can tell you without a doubt that it's more fun helping others win than winning myself. Marianne Williamson was right when she said, "Success means we go to sleep at night knowing that our talents and abilities were used in a way that served others." I now find great value in adding value to others.

Serving others purifies our motives. Doing things well for the right reason gives great value to us. So every time I add value, I gain value. As Dieter F. Uchtdorf said, "As we lose ourselves in the service of others, we discover our own lives and our own happiness."

7. The Giftedness Question: "What do I do best that allows me to serve people best?"

As leaders, we serve others best in the areas where we are most gifted. As I look back on my life, I can see that the best leaders I had used their gifts to bring out the best in me. That started with my father. Not only did he use his gift of encouragement to inspire me and give me confidence, he also used his relational connections to introduce me to influential leaders and equip me for leadership.

Another person who helped me was my mentor Tom Phillippe. When I was in my early thirties, and had an opportunity to make a career transition, Tom, who was a fantastic businessman, took over my little fledgling business to keep it from dying until I once again had enough time to take it back. Tom and my father are just two of many leaders who have used their best gifts to serve me.

I've tried to do the same for others. My greatest gifts are in speaking, writing, and mentoring. Not only does my speaking serve the people I teach, but it also helps my companies by connecting me to other leaders and organizations. And I've made it a regular practice to mentor up-and-coming leaders. An hour or two with a high-potential leader a couple of times a year can help them answer critical leadership questions and assist them in navigating issues where I have some experience.

Think about what you do best that will allow you to serve others best. Use these questions to help you:

- What are my strengths? How can I use them to serve others?
- What is my background? How can I use it to serve others?
- What are my experiences? How can I use them to serve others?
- What are my opportunities? How can I use them to serve others?
- What do I love? How can I use it to serve others?
- Where am I growing? How can I use that to serve others?

The leaders who work with me are striving to serve others with their best gifts. Mark Cole is good with people, so he spends most of his time there. Paul Martinelli, the president of the John Maxwell Team, my organization that trains speakers and coaches, is best at strategic production, so he serves others by figuring out how to continually grow and improve the organization. Meridith Simes has a fantastic mind for marketing, so she is helping my organizations connect with people so they have access to resources they need. Whatever you do best is what you should use to serve others most.

8. THE EXAMPLE QUESTION: "HOW CAN I SERVE PEOPLE IN A WAY THAT WILL INSPIRE THEM TO SERVE OTHERS?"

Recently I hosted a meeting at the Breakers resort in Palm Beach. It's a beautiful facility, and the service is excellent. While I was there, I struck up a conversation with executive vice president and chief sales and marketing officer David Burke, and he told me about the organization's focus on service. "Servant leadership is at the core of everything we do here at the Breakers," he said. "Every new team member goes through a two-day orientation prior to beginning their normal duties. During half of the final day of the orientation process, the new hires accompany a senior executive to go out and perform four to five hours of community service at one of the many organizations around the county: Urban Youth Impact, Homeless Coalition, Food Bank, the Lord's Place, ARC, and so on. We serve not only our guests, but each other and the community.

We pay our employees to go out on their days off to perform community service."

David said he believes that what they do for the community is their legacy and more important than financial results. I love that. And I love that their senior executives lead the charge as they serve people.

As a leader, I am always very conscious of the example I set for everyone I lead and serve. And that often prompts me to be more open and vulnerable than I otherwise might be. When I was getting ready to turn sixty, I spent some time thinking about who I wanted to be as I entered what felt like a new stage of life. So after spending some time with God, I wrote a prayer to Him about who I hoped He would help me to become. I'm very aware of my shortcomings, and I wanted God's help to please Him and to become more like Jesus, who was not above serving others, even doing the menial work of washing His disciples' feet.

I wrote the prayer for myself, but I quickly felt prompted to share it with others, even though it reveals some of my personal struggles. And I share it with you now in the hope that it helps you. My prayer at sixty was this:

> Lord, as I grow older, I would like to be known as . . .
> Available—rather than a hard worker.
> Compassionate—more than competent.
> Content—not driven.
> Generous—instead of rich.
> Gentle—over being powerful.
> Listener—more than a great communicator.
> Loving—versus quick or bright.
> Reliable—not famous.
> Sacrificial—instead of successful.
> Self-controlled—rather than exciting.
> Thoughtful—more than gifted.
> I want to be a foot washer!

More than ten years have passed since I wrote that prayer. I'm now in my seventies, and I'm still working to become the servant I desire to be. I have a long way to go, but I'm giving it my all.

Why you lead and the way you lead are important. They define you, your leadership, and ultimately your contribution. By humbling yourself and "stepping down" from your position, and by making service to others a core part of your leadership values, you, ironically, raise your game, because you help and empower others. Perhaps that's why Chinese philosopher Lao-Tzu wrote, "The highest type of ruler is one of whose existence the people are barely aware. . . . The Sage is self-effacing and scanty of words. When his task is accomplished and things have been completed, all the people say, 'We ourselves have achieved it.'"[11]

DEVELOPING THE *SERVANT* WITHIN YOU

To become a leader who serves others, you need to focus on making changes in two areas.

DEVELOP THE HEART OF A SERVANT

Servant leadership develops from the inside out. People can sense your attitude toward them. They can tell if you look down on them or want to raise them up. They know if you want to help them or hinder them in order to help yourself. They sense whether you are a ladder climber or a ladder builder. That's why serving others has to begin in your heart.

Do you genuinely care about people and want to help them be their best? Do you want others to succeed *at least* as much as you want to succeed yourself? Most of us are selfish (me included). We each have to work at developing a servant's heart. If you need help with the process, you may want to try doing the things I mention in the chapter:

1. ***Don't Rely on Your Position or Title:*** How must you change how you lead to meet people on common ground instead of relying on position?
2. ***Believe in People and Their Potential:*** How can you encourage the success of people around you, even those you don't like?

3. *See Things from the Perspective of Others:* How can you connect with someone who rubs you the wrong way or leaves you cold to learn his or her perspective?

4. *Create an Environment of Encouragement:* What positive things can you say every day to the people on your team to motivate and inspire them?

5. *Measure Your Success by How Much Value You Add to Others:* What must you change so that you measure the success of your day by how *others* succeed?

Start with these changes, and see how much your attitude improves.

Develop the Hands of a Servant

A change of heart is like gratitude. If it is unexpressed, it has little value. As you seek to develop the heart of a servant, be sure to follow through with the *actions* of a servant. Wake up every morning thinking about how you can help the members of your team succeed—personally, professionally, developmentally, relationally, and so forth. If you make them better or more successful in any way, you're on the right track.

EIGHT

THE INDISPENSABLE QUALITY OF LEADERSHIP:
VISION

Vision *is* the indispensable quality of leadership. Without it, a team's energy ebbs, people begin to miss deadlines, team members' personal agendas begin to dominate, production falls, and eventually team members scatter. With it, the team's energy surges, people meet their deadlines, personal agendas fade into the background, production increases, and the people working together become a thriving team.

As my friend Andy Stanley said, "Vision gives significance to the otherwise meaningless details of our lives. . . . Too many times the routines of life begin to feel like shoveling dirt. But take those same routines, those same responsibilities, and view them through the lens of vision and everything looks different. Vision brings your world into focus. Vision brings order to chaos. A clear vision enables you to see everything differently."[1]

Clear vision does wonders for a team, but it also does wonders for a leader. Among its greatest benefits are direction and passion. For leaders, vision sets direction for their lives. It's like having a road map. It prioritizes both action and values, helping leaders remain focused. And it creates passion. It lights a fire within leaders that can spread to others. As my friend Bill Hybels has said, "Vision is a picture of the future that produces passion. There is no such thing as an 'emotionless vision.'" Perhaps that's why Helen Keller, when asked what would be worse than being born blind, answered, "To have sight without vision."

VISION STATEMENTS

All leaders have one thing in common. They see more and before others. What makes that indispensable is that it allows their followers to begin expanding their vision and acting on it more quickly. If the leader doesn't see the vision, the people never will.

Why is vision so important for a leader? Why must you be able to see what others can't? There are many reasons:

1. What You Can See Determines What You Can Be

I have often wondered about whether the vision makes the leader or if the leader makes the vision. After years of thinking about this and observing leaders, I believe the vision comes first. I have known many leaders who lost the vision and, accordingly, lost their power to lead.

People do what people see. That is the greatest motivational principle in the world. In other words, people depend on the leader for visual stimulation and direction. And when it comes to vision, I believe there are four kinds of people that leaders encounter:

- People who never see it—they are wanderers.
- People who see it but never pursue it on their own—they are followers.
- People who see it and pursue it—they are achievers.
- People who see it, pursue it, and help others see and pursue it—they are leaders.

The vast majority of people fall into the first two categories. They do not pursue a dream on their own. And those who are willing to follow don't go after the dream directly; they follow leaders who possess a dream and who have the ability to communicate it effectively. That's why it's so important for a leader to nurture a dream or vision and take responsibility for it. Only when that happens can the vision grow and the leader attract a following. Couple a vision with a leader willing to implement that dream, and a movement begins.

When I was a teenager, I read *As a Man Thinketh* by James Allen. It had a major impact on me and helped to begin awakening the leader within me. Allen said, "The dreamers are the saviors of the world." That really stirred my desire to dream big, and I began to wonder how I could help others in a big way.

I came away from reading Allen's book with two great lessons. First, I needed to cherish my ideals. Allen wrote:

Cherish your visions. Cherish your ideals. Cherish the music that stirs in your heart, the beauty that forms in your mind, the loveliness that drapes your purest thoughts, for out of them will grow all delightful conditions, all heavenly environment; of these, if you but remain true to them, your world will at last be built.[2]

Second, I needed to mine for the gold. Allen wrote, "Only by much searching and mining are gold and diamonds obtained, and man can find every truth connected with his being if he will dig deep into the mine of his soul."[3] The vision we embrace as leaders comes from within us, from our best thoughts and noblest ideals, but we have to work to bring them to the surface. Having vision as a leader is *my* responsibility.

2. YOU SEE ONLY WHAT YOU ARE PREPARED TO SEE

German statesman Konrad Adenauer said, "We all live under the same sky but we don't all have the same horizon." Everyone has the potential to possess vision, but not everyone does. And that's a function of their perspective.

In *A Savior for All Seasons*, William Barker relates the story of a bishop from the East Coast who paid a visit to a small, Midwestern religious college around the beginning of

> We all live under the same sky but we don't all have the same horizon.
>
> —KONRAD ADENAUER

the twentieth century. He stayed at the home of the college president, who also served as the college's professor of physics and chemistry. After dinner, the bishop mentioned that he thought just about everything in nature had been discovered and all inventions had been conceived.

The college president politely disagreed and said he felt there would be many more discoveries. When the bishop challenged the president to name just one such invention, the president replied he was certain that within fifty years men would be able to fly.

"Nonsense!" replied the bishop. "Only angels are intended to fly."

The bishop's name was Milton Wright, and he had two boys at home—Orville and Wilbur—who would prove to have greater vision than their father.[4] The father and his sons both lived under the same sky, but they didn't all have the same horizon.

If we want to possess a vision for our leadership, we need to prepare for it. We need to anticipate it. When we possess positive anticipation and are excited about what's ahead, we're highly motivated and we prepare diligently. When we do this consistently, our sense of anticipation becomes the catalyst for inspiration.

3. What You See Is What You Get

The third thing you need to know about vision, in addition to knowing that what you see determines what you can be and what you see is what you are prepared to see, is that what you receive is largely based on what you perceive. Leaders understand that they have to believe it to see it, while most people go through life saying, "I have to see it to believe it."

A great illustration of this concept is contained in Luis Palau's book *Dream Great Dreams*. Palau wrote:

> Think about how nice and refreshing it is to taste a cold Coke. Hundreds of millions of people around the world have enjoyed this experience, thanks to the vision of Robert Woodruff. During his tenure as president of Coca-Cola (1923–1955), Woodruff boldly declared, "We will see that every man in uniform get a bottle of Coca-Cola for five cents wherever he is and whatever the costs." When World War II had ended, Woodruff

stated that before he died he wanted every person in the world to have tasted Coca-Cola. Robert Woodruff was a man of vision!

With careful planning and a lot of persistence, Woodruff and his colleagues reached their generation and around the globe for Coke.

When Disney World first opened, Mrs. Walt Disney was asked to speak at the Grand Opening, since Walt had died. She was introduced by a man who said, "Mrs. Disney, I just wish Walt could have seen this." She stood up and said, "He did," and sat down. Walt Disney knew it. Robert Woodruff knew it. Even Flip Wilson knew it! What you see is what you get.[5]

As a leader, you must strive to see more and before others do. You need to have aspirations. You must be the opposite of what author Kenneth Hildebrand called the "mundane man," whom he described as believing "only what he sees, only what is immediate, only what he can put his hands on." He went on to say:

The mundane man lacks depth. He lacks vision. The poorest of all men is not the one without a nickel to his name. He is the fellow without a dream. The mundane man resembles a great ship made for the mighty ocean but trying to navigate in a millpond. He has no far port to reach, no lifting horizon, no precious cargo to carry. His hours are absorbed in routine and petty tyrannies. Small wonder if he gets dissatisfied, quarrelsome and "fed up." One of life's greatest tragedies is a person with 10-by-12 capacity and a two-by-four soul.[6]

Good leaders don't allow themselves to be dragged down into mundane territory. They set their eyes to the horizon and their hearts on the people. They know that a lot depends on their vision. That's why my friend, Pastor Rick Warren, echoing the advice of one

> If you want to know the temperature of your organization, you should put a thermometer in the leader's mouth.
>
> —RICK WARREN

of his professors, advises that if you want to know the temperature of your organization, you should put a thermometer in the leader's mouth.[7] Leaders can't take their people farther than they can see. That's why their vision needs to be clear.

HOW TO INCREASE YOUR "MORE AND BEFORE"

Author Napoleon Hill said, "Cherish your visions and dreams as they are the children of your soul: the blueprints of your ultimate achievements."[8] Good leaders see more and before others, and they work to increase that capacity on an ongoing basis. That may seem like a challenge. Many people believe that either you have it or you don't. I disagree with that. I believe everyone has the capacity to improve in this area. Here's how:

1. KNOW THERE IS MORE "MORE AND BEFORE" OUT THERE

My life has been one of continual vision expansion. Adding value to people was the birth of my vision. Today that vision has taken many forms and has expanded far beyond my initial hopes and dreams. As I reflect, I can think of two distinct times when I was tempted to think there was no more "more and before" in my vision.

The first was at the beginning of my career during the birth of my original dream of growing a church that could help people. My dream was at its most vulnerable at that time. Why? Because the vision was new to me. I had no track record of success in realizing a vision, and I lacked the experience needed to overcome the vision challenges before me. In addition, I was susceptible to the opinions of my friends. If they were negative, and many were, I was in danger of dismissing the "more and before" I envisioned within me, and I might just dismiss it as unattainable. I wish back then I would have known a quote by Jonas Salk, the developer of the polio vaccine. He said, "First people will tell you that you are wrong. Then they will tell you that you are right, but what you're doing really isn't important. Finally, they will admit that you are right and that what you are doing is very important; but after all, they knew it all the time."[9]

The second time I was tempted to give up on increasing my ability to see more and before occurred when I was in my midforties. I had established myself professionally in my third church, I had an influential position, and I could have been set for life. I felt as if I were living on the mountaintop. What would I do? Settle in? Or keep striving?

Psychologist Judith Meyerowitz said that something happens to many people at around age forty-five. They lose the vision of a greater future for themselves. Some people stop working and begin fantasizing instead.[10] I didn't want to do that. I didn't want to be satisfied with the mountain I had climbed. I looked around for a higher mountaintop and struck out for it.

Today two qualities help keep me focused on ways to increase my "more and before:" creativity and flexibility. Harnessing creativity helps me to believe there is always an answer. That mind-set enables me to see things before others do because I expect to. Flexibility reminds me that there is always more than one answer. That mind-set enables me to see more than others see. These two concepts greatly influence how I see the future. They allow me to think with abundance and not scarcity. They convince me that there are no hopeless situations, only people who think hopelessly.

I encourage you to embrace those two qualities. And never allow someone else to determine your vision. If they do, chances are they will make it too small.

2. DEVELOP A PROCESS FOR FINDING MORE "MORE AND BEFORE"

The Law of Design in *The 15 Invaluable Laws of Growth* says, "To maximize growth, develop strategies."[11] That concept works as well for vision as it does for personal growth. Because strategies are nothing more than systems for obtaining specific results, they are like freeways. They can help you quickly get to where you want to go.

In chapter 6 I wrote about the process Paul Martinelli uses to put attitude into action: Test → Fail → Learn → Improve → Reenter. That is also a great process to increase the "more and before" in your vision.

- **Test:** Get out of your comfort zone by sharing your vision. On whom can you test it to see if there is a positive response? Where can you share it that you haven't before? You never know who might benefit from your vision until you test it.

- **Fail:** Failure allows you to find out what doesn't work. That's so important. You won't eliminate what doesn't work until you know it doesn't. Why don't we do that more?
- **Learn:** A teachable spirit plus humility fosters the learning experience that is essential for expanding your vision.
- **Improve:** As a leader, you need to continually ask yourself, "Am I getting better?" That is the question on every successful person's mind each day. That is the road to improvement.
- **Reenter:** None of this matters unless you get back into the game. The person who falls and gets right back up may be admired for his tenacity, but that does little good unless he learns, improves, and applies what he learns.

Warren Bennis said, "Leadership is the capacity to translate vision into reality."[12] The process I just outlined will help you do exactly that.

3. Spend Time with People Who Inspire You to See "More and Before"

In chapter 5 I mentioned that author Jim Collins taught me about a concept that he called "who luck," the idea that the people you know make a huge difference in your life. I believe who luck is the most important luck of all. I can look back on my life and verify what a difference it makes. Back in 1971, as a young pastor, I called the pastors of the ten largest churches in America and asked for a thirty-minute appointment to ask them questions about their leadership and success. Two of the ten said yes, and my who-luck journey began. My conversations with them helped me to see more and before. And those two leaders helped me meet the other eight who had originally said no.

> Leadership is the capacity to translate vision into reality.
>
> —WARREN BENNIS

I can point to time after time in my life when I was around people who expanded my vision and made me want to be more than I was. And since meeting those two leaders, I have intentionally sought out people and experiences that would stretch my leadership gifts and enlarge my vision. And here's what I've discovered:

- When I'm with the right people and in the right places, I don't spend time; I invest it. This is where I get my greatest ROI.
- Who luck is 90 percent intentional and 10 percent accidental. You can't just *hope* to meet people who will stretch you. Hope is not a strategy.
- It is impossible to be around bigger people and not become bigger yourself. These kinds of experiences can change your life.
- The best way to meet the right people is by asking the right question: "Who do you know that I should know?"
- Preparation beforehand and reflection afterward maximize these experiences.
- Including members of my team is the best way for us to grow together. Whenever possible, take people with you.
- The second meeting with the right person is the most important meeting. It indicates that both of you see the value of meeting again, and that perhaps it is the beginning of an ongoing relationship.

Are you actively searching for people who can enlarge you and your vision? Is it one of your top priorities? If it's not, it should be.

4. Ask Questions That Will Help You Increase Your "More and Before"

In my book *Good Leaders Ask Great Questions*, I wrote that questions are the keys that unlock the doors of opportunity.[13] While in New York City recently, I was asked by an interviewer, "What is the greatest difference between your leadership in your thirties and today?" After a moment of reflection, I replied, "In my thirties I gave a lot of direction. Today I ask a lot of questions."

When we find our vision, we find our way. However, there is another discovery that is equally important—the people who will join us on the journey to fulfill that vision. Questions allow us to get to know people when we meet them and whether we should take that trip together. Questions also open the door for the exchange of great ideas, which will help to shape and inform your vision.

Leading by assumption usually ends up to be a leadership nightmare. The right questions kill wrong assumptions. The more successful the person you meet, the better your questions need to be. And the better the answers you will receive.

5. Intentionally Grow Every Day to Increase Your Capacity for "More and Before"

Personal growth is my passion because it has continually enlarged my capacity and my vision. Many years ago, when I heard Earl Nightingale say, "If a person will spend one hour a day every day for five years on a certain subject, that person will become an expert on that subject," I determined to follow his advice in the area of leadership. So for one hour a day, every day, I studied leadership.

For the first two years I kept asking myself, "How long will it take?" I wanted to "arrive" as an expert. But then something wonderful happened. I began to experience the joy of personal growth. I could see my progress. Better yet, others could too. That's when I fell in love with the journey of growing. And my question changed from "How long will it take?" to "How far can I go?" I've been asking myself that same question for the last forty-five years. I haven't found the answer yet, and I don't think I will. Don't think I want to. I'm still growing, and I love it.

> If you are working on something exciting that you really care about, you don't have to be pushed. The vision pulls you.
>
> —STEVE JOBS

Steve Jobs said, "If you are working on something exciting that you really care about, you don't have to be pushed. The vision pulls you." He's right. I still feel the pull of personal growth, and it is taking me forward as a leader.

PERSONAL OWNERSHIP OF THE VISION

In my book *Put Your Dreams to the Test*, one of the questions I ask has to do with ownership: Is my dream really my dream? Why? Because you cannot achieve a dream that you do not own.[14] Take a look at the differences you will experience based on whether or not you own your dream:

When Someone Else Owns Your Dream	When You Own Your Dream
It will not have the right fit.	It will feel good on you.
It will be a weight on your shoulders.	It will provide wings to your spirit.
It will drain your energy.	It will fire you up.
It will put you to sleep.	It will keep you up at night.
It will take you out of your strength zone.	It will take you out of your comfort zone.
It will be fulfilling to others.	It will be fulfilling to you.
It will require others to make you do it.	It will feel like you were made for it.

You will never achieve a dream or vision unless you own it. Furthermore, as a leader, you will not be able to get others to buy into a vision that you do not own.

Through the years, one of the most common questions I've been asked at leadership conferences is "How do I get a vision for my organization?" When I hear this question, I feel for the leader who asks it, because I know it means the person has been placed in a leadership position yet lacks this indispensable quality of leadership. Until the vision question is answered, the person will be a leader in name only. I hope that you already possess a vision of your own for your team, department, or organization. However, if you don't, I want to help you. Although I cannot give you a vision, I can share the process of seeking one for yourself and those around you. And I can help you think through the process of implementing it.

LOOK WITHIN YOU: "WHAT DO YOU FEEL?"

You cannot borrow somebody else's vision. It must come from inside you. What brings it out is passion. What fires you up? What is so important to you that it keeps you up at night, makes your blood boil, or gives you great joy? Those are vision clues.

One of the leaders I admire most is Winston Churchill. Whenever I visit London, I go to the Churchill War Rooms, the underground offices where the prime minister and other British leaders made their plans for fighting against the Nazis during World War II. Against great odds, Churchill led Great Britain through some of its darkest hours, inspiring millions of people to "never, never, never give up!" He said, "Before you can inspire with emotion, you must be swamped with it yourself. Before you can move their tears, your own must flow. To convince them, you must yourself believe."

When seeking vision, why is it important to start on the inside? There are three main reasons. First, there will be pressure from outside of you that could dilute the vision or distract you from it. You may receive a vision for free, but the journey to fulfill that vision never is. Every day someone or something will stand in the way of where your vision wants to take you. The obstacles and opposition are constant. They can wear you down. The result? Often, vision "leaks." When it does, the strength within you is what you must draw upon to sustain you.

Second, a vision birthed within you rings true and has authenticity when it is shared with others. Former president of Notre Dame University Theodore Hesburgh said, "A vision must be articulated clearly and forcefully on every occasion. You can't blow an uncertain trumpet." An "uncertain trumpet" is usually the result of a leader trying to cast someone else's vision without deep conviction.

And finally, only a vision that comes from within possesses the "weight" needed to do something significant. Visions without weight are easily dismissed and discarded. Easy come, easy go. A vision with weight does not feel optional; it is essential. It carries opportunities but also consequences if ignored by the leader. Weighty visions are ever present for leaders who possess them. And the weight of that vision can become like their North Star. It guides them. It

> Your vision will become clear only when you look into your heart. Who looks outside, dreams. Who looks inside, awakens.
>
> —CARL JUNG

gives them credibility. It gives them gravitas. And it gives them joy in the journey. A vision without weight is often a delusion. A weight without a vision often leads to depression.

Psychiatrist Carl Jung said, "Your vision will become clear only when you look into your heart. Who looks outside, dreams. Who looks inside, awakens." Look inside yourself, pay attention to how you feel, and begin to awaken to your dream, your vision as a leader.

Look Behind You: "What have you learned?"

Every significant vision possessed by leaders is built upon their past—the lessons they've learned, the pain they've experienced, the significant observations they've made. For example, when I started my career as a pastor, I believed I was supposed to focus much of my time and attention on administrative duties. The models of leadership I had observed growing up focused their attention on this area. But I quickly discovered that I had no talent and even less patience for administration. It didn't matter how hard or how long I worked at it. I became very frustrated. Finally, I had to admit that I wasn't going to get any better, and I needed to find other ways for the essential administrative duties of the church to be accomplished other than doing them myself. I soon began enlisting the help of volunteers who were skilled at administration and who were fulfilled by it. And in my second church, I was able to hire an administrative assistant. Oh happy day!

I learned my lesson in that first leadership position. If you were to look back at the way I've led every organization since then, you'd see that I didn't even *attempt* to take on an administrative role. I left that to people who were skilled in that area. It has freed me up to be a better leader. I focus on my strengths.

What experiences from your past inform your vision? What have your successes—and especially your failures—taught you about life and leadership? These things need to be part of your vision as a leader.

Look Around You: "What is happening to others?"

Once the vision is birthed within you, you must pay attention to the people you want to help you implement it. Why? The Law of Buy-In in *The*

21 Irrefutable Laws of Leadership states, "People buy into the leader, then the vision." If you don't get people's buy-in, the vision will not go anywhere.

Good leaders watch the people to know how and when to present the vision. They listen to the people, learn from the people, and then discern how to lead the people. They pay attention to timing because, as the Law of Timing says, "When to lead is as important as what to do and where to go."[15]

When it comes to timing, I love the story of the little boy who attended his first symphonic concert. He was excited by the splendid hall, the people in their finery, and the music of the professional orchestra. Of all the instruments, his favorite were the cymbals. Their first dramatic crash captivated him. But then he noticed that the cymbal player mostly stood motionless and only occasionally made his musical contribution. And even then it was quite brief.

After the concert, the little boy's parents took him backstage to meet some of the musicians. The boy immediately sought out the percussionist who played the cymbals.

"How much do you need to know to play the cymbals?" he asked.

The musician laughed and answered, "For the cymbals, you don't have to know much. You only have to know when."

A good idea can become great when the people are ready. Leaders who are impatient with people and try to force an idea before it's accepted will be frustrated in their efforts to see their vision become reality. The evidence of leadership strength lies not in forcefully streaking ahead, but in adapting your stride to the slower pace of others while not forfeiting your leadership. As leaders, if we run too far ahead, we lose our power to influence people.

Look Above You: "What does God expect of you?"

Before I move on to the next and final place to look to define and create personal ownership of your dream, I want to tell you how God comes into play in my life. I do this because I am a person of faith, and to be true to myself and how vision works in my life, I must include God. If this offends you, please just skip this section and go to the next point.

I believe God's gift to me is my potential. My gift back to God is what I do with that potential. I believe great leaders sense a higher calling, one that lifts them above the crowd. It compels them to try to achieve something meaningful, something significant for others. To people of faith, that calling is God ordained.

What a terrible waste of life it would be to climb the ladder of success only to find when you reached the top that it was leaning against the wrong building. That's why I ask God to direct me. It's why my definition of success is

- Knowing God and His desires for me.
- Growing to my maximum potential.
- Sowing seeds that benefit others.

If you desire God's help with your vision and calling, simply ask Him to help you. I've even encouraged my atheist friends to do this. Try it, and see what happens.

Look Ahead of You: "What is the big picture?"

If you've paid attention to what you feel, what you've learned, what's happening to others, what resources are available to you, and what God expects of you, then you're ready to look at the big picture. This is the last thought for the making of a vision.

Recently I was doing a podcast for Growing Leaders, an organization led by my friend Tim Elmore. The theme was "Fast-Forward." The interviewer asked me for my thoughts on that theme, and it got me thinking about the ever-increasing speed of life. As we look forward, we see the future coming faster, not slower. The older I get, the more I think life is like a roll of toilet paper. The closer to the end you get, the faster it goes!

The big picture was easier to see fifty years ago when I started as a leader. Back then we were encouraged to have long-range plans (ten years), middle-range plans (five years), and short-range plans (one to two years). Today in many companies, a long-range plan may be only two years because the need to change and adapt is so strong. With that kind of pace, a leader's ability to see more than others and before others allows him or her not to be fixated on what is now, but to focus on what will be in the future. When I started as a leader, seeing more was more important than seeing before. Today I think that is changing. Seeing before others see is essential to success as a leader. Today there are often no first-, second-, and third-place finishers. There's just whoever finishes first. Everyone else is out of the game.

PAINT A PICTURE OF THE VISION FOR THEM

If you understand the value of vision, are dedicated to seeing more and before others, and have done the sometimes hard work of discovering and developing a vision, then what? Nothing will happen unless you are willing and able to paint a clear picture of your vision for people and mobilize them to join you. As my friend Andy Stanley says, if the vision isn't clear, then the mist in your mind will eventually become a fog in your organization.[16]

> If the vision isn't clear, then the mist in your mind will eventually become a fog in your organization.
>
> —ANDY STANLEY

A picture of your vision is worth a thousand words, since people think and remember in pictures. Often leaders do this verbally. Author Donald T. Phillips, who has extensively studied leaders and orators, said, "Of all human senses, sound is the primary intellectual stimulant— while vision is secondary. A speech combines both sound *and* vision and, therefore, can be an unusually effective method of communication to a mass audience."[17]

Every great vision has certain components, and the best leaders make sure they include these in the picture so their people experience them.

THE HORIZON

A leader's vision of the distant horizon allows people to see the heights of their possibilities. While it's true that the individuals you connect with will determine how far or high they want to go, it's your responsibility as the leader to put plenty of sky into the picture. Paul Harvey said that a blind man's world is bounded by the limits of his touch; an ignorant man's world by the limits of his knowledge; a great man's world by the limits of his vision. As a visionary leader painting a picture of the future for people, you can expand their horizons.

THE SUN

Everyone desires warmth and hope. When you paint a bright future for people, they feel the warmth. And they feel the optimism that comes from the "light" you provide. A prime function of every leader is to keep hope alive.

MOUNTAINS

Every vision has its challenges. Edwin Land, founder of Polaroid, said, "The first thing you do is teach the person to feel that the vision is very important and nearly impossible. That draws out the drive in the winner."

As a leader, don't pretend the challenges don't exist. People will see through your deception. Instead, acknowledge those challenges and obstacles, and assure the people you are all in it together and will conquer them as a team.

BIRDS

Watching an eagle rise causes people to feel their own spirits soar. People need this kind of inspiration. They need to be reminded of the power of the human spirit to rise up. As General George S. Patton said, "Wars may be fought with weapons, but they are won by men. It is the spirit of the men who follow and of the man who leads that gains the victory."[18]

FLOWERS

Achieving a great vision takes time. It takes great energy and effort. It can't be accomplished in one great push. For that reason, you need to allow people to stop and smell the flowers along the way. They need rest stops, where they can be refreshed mentally, emotionally, and physically.

Trust me—my natural inclination is to just keep pressing forward. I had to learn to allow people to breathe when they need it.

The Path

People need direction. They want a path to follow. And they want to know that you know the way forward, that you can take them from where they are to the place they want to go. You must be like the Native American guide who, when asked how he was able to lead the way over jagged peaks, through forests, and along treacherous trails, answered, "I have the near look and the far vision. With the one I see what is directly ahead of me; with the other I guide my course by the stars."

Yourself

Never paint the vision without placing yourself in the picture. This will show your commitment to the vision and your desire to walk alongside your people through the entire process. You are not only the guide but the model to follow, and the person to lend a hand when they need to be helped to climb. As onetime United Nations ambassador Warren R. Austin said, "If you would lift me, you must be on higher ground."

The Things the People Love

> If you would lift me, you must be on higher ground.
>
> —WARREN R. AUSTIN

Never forget that people are motivated most by who and what they love. And that's why we need to remember to include these things in the picture we paint. That's what was done in the parachute factories during World War II. Parachutes needed to be constructed by the thousands, but it was a tedious job. It involved crouching over a sewing machine eight to ten hours a day and stitching endless lengths of monochromatic fabric. Even as sewers made progress on a parachute, what they worked on looked like a formless heap of cloth.

How did the leaders combat the boredom and prevent the potential mistakes? Every morning workers were reminded that each stitch they made was part of a lifesaving operation. They were asked to think as they sewed that each parachute might be the one worn by their husband, brother, or son. Although the work was hard and the hours long, the women and the men on the home front understood their contribution to the larger picture. They were fulfilling a vision that helped the ones they loved most.

I love the way Columbus challenged prevailing wisdom through his bold actions. When he set sail westward into the Atlantic Ocean, the flag of Spain under which he traveled bore the motto *Ne Plus Ultra*, meaning "Nothing Farther." Traditionally those words described Spain's Straits of Gibraltar, also known as the Pillars of Hercules. But after Columbus's journeys and his discovery of the New World, Charles V of Spain changed the nation's motto to *Plus Ultra*, meaning "Farther Beyond" or "Something More." The entire nation—and in fact the entire Western world—changed and mobilized its resources, because people's vision of the world changed.

Apple cofounder Steve Jobs said, "The only way to do great work is to love what you do. If you haven't found it yet, keep looking. Don't settle. As with all matters of the heart, you'll know when you find it."[19] As a leader, when you discover your vision, it becomes your fire, your inspiration, and your guide. If you haven't found it yet, don't give up. Keep looking. You'll know it when you find it. And when you do, nurture it, embrace it, own it, and paint a compelling picture of it to others. Because vision is the indispensable quality of leadership. Without it, you will never develop the leader within you to the fullest.

DEVELOPING THE *VISIONARY* WITHIN YOU

Since vision is the indispensable quality of leadership, you don't want to find yourself in a leadership position or with leadership responsibilities without it.

IDENTIFY YOUR VISION

If you don't have a clear vision for your leadership, then spend some time asking and answering the five questions contained in the chapter:

Look Within You: What Do You Feel?
Look Behind You: What Have You Learned?
Look Around You: What Is Happening to Others?
Look Above You: What Does God Expect of You?
Look Ahead of You: What Is the Big Picture?

INCREASE YOUR VISION

Do you see more and before the people you lead? Do you have a handle on the big picture and see problems before others do? Or are you often blindsided? Do you have to be told by your people about the problems and challenges ahead?

If you're not ahead of your people, you will eventually lose your value as a leader to them. You need to improve your ability to see more and before. To do that, focus on these three areas:

- *Spend Time with People Who Inspire You to Dream Bigger:* Who do you know who thinks and dreams big? Ask for a meeting with the person or to just tag along when you can.
- *Ask Questions to Help You See Farther and Wider:* Don't take things at face value. Cultivate an inquiring mind. Get out of your comfort zone.
- *Develop a Vision Growth Plan:* What can you do to grow in the area of vision? Can you read biographies of great leaders and innovators? Do you need to expand your technical capabilities? Should you expose yourself to other cultures? Stretch your thinking and your expectations. Learn to think bigger.

NINE

THE PRICE TAG OF LEADERSHIP:

SELF-DISCIPLINE

President Harry S. Truman said, "In reading the lives of great men, I have found that the first victory they won was over themselves. . . . Self-discipline with all of them came first." That is true not just of great achievers, but also of effective leaders. Good leaders practice self-control before they try to engage others. Self-discipline comes before leadership success. It is the price tag of leadership.

When I was in college, I studied Greek and Hebrew. One of the words for self-control in Greek is *egkráteia*. I think this word gives great insight into what someone needs to lead effectively. The word means to get a grip on oneself.[1] It describes people who are willing to get a grip on their lives and take control of areas that will bring them success or failure. That's critical because I need to get a grip on me first before I try to get a handle on leading others.

As leaders, our greatest challenge in leadership is leading ourselves first. We can't expect to take others farther than we have gone ourselves. We must travel within before we can travel without. Many highly gifted leaders have stopped far short of their potential because they were not willing to pay this price. They tried to take the fast track to leadership only to find that shortcuts never pay off in the long run.

SELF-DISCIPLINE MAKES LEADERSHIP'S UPHILL CLIMB POSSIBLE

There is a truth you need to recognize, not just for leadership, but for everything in life. For the last year or so I have been teaching it extensively to people wherever I go. Ready? Here it is. *Everything worthwhile is uphill.*

You may be saying, "Now that you've pointed it out, I can see that. Good. Okay. Let's move on. What's next?" But I want you to stop for a minute and think about this. *Everything* worthwhile is uphill. The word *everything* is inclusive. It's all-encompassing. Pair that with *worthwhile*— the things that are desirable, appropriate, good for you, attractive, beneficial. So when you think about that, it's very significant. Anything and everything you desire in life, everything you would like to strive for, is *uphill*, meaning the pursuit of it is challenging, grueling, exhausting, strenuous, and difficult.

As leaders, our greatest challenge in leadership is leading ourselves first.

The implications are simple: there are no such things as accidental achievements. No person who has climbed the mountain of success ever said, "I have no idea how I got to the top of this mountain. I just woke up one day, and here I was." No leader who ever led people to do something significant did it without great effort. Any climb uphill must be deliberate, consistent, and willful. It is very intentional.

The statement "Everything worthwhile is uphill" not only describes life, but explains the reason self-discipline is so essential for a successful life. And that's why I want to spend this chapter explaining some truths about self-discipline, because if you embrace them and act on them, you will be empowered to live an exciting uphill journey, and you will be able to pay the price tag of leadership. So let's get started.

1. SELF-DISCIPLINE ENABLES YOU TO GO UPHILL

If I were to ask you, "Do you want to improve your life?" of course your answer would be yes. The question isn't *if* you want it to happen.

The question is *how* do you make it happen? The answer is by living each day with intentionality. That requires becoming self-disciplined.

Self-discipline moves you from good intentions to good actions. It is what separates words and ideas from actual results. One of the greatest gaps in life is between sounding good and doing good. We are ultimately measured by what we do and how our actions shape the world around us. Without results, all the best intentions in the world are just a way of at best entertaining ourselves, at worst deluding ourselves. Self-discipline paves the road to results.

Everything worthwhile is uphill.

Do you know people who are always getting ready to get ready? Do you know people who start but never finish? I do too. They need to heed the advice of poet Edgar A. Guest, who wrote a poem called "Keep Going." It says:

> When things go wrong, as they sometimes will,
> And the road you're trudging seems all up hill,
> When the funds are low and the debts are high,
> And you want to smile, but you have to sigh,
> When care is pressing you down a bit,
> Rest, if you must—but don't you quit.
> Life is queer with its twists and turns,
> As every one of us sometimes learns,
> And many a failure turns about
> When he might have won had he stuck it out.
> Don't give up though the pace seems slow—
> You may succeed with another blow.
> Success is failure turned inside out—
> The silver tint of the clouds of doubt,
> And you never can tell how close you are,
> It may be near when it seems far;
> So stick to the fight when you're hardest hit—
> It's when things seem worst that you mustn't quit.[2]

As a young leader, when I was highly focused on developing self-discipline, I would often think and talk about what I was going through.

I felt the difficulty of the leadership tasks I was taking on, I felt the difficulty of making the uphill climb, and I wanted the people around me to know I was willing to pay the price to improve. Maybe back then I hoped I would come to a place where I didn't have to keep climbing. But that's not the way it works. Today I am still climbing. But the self-discipline needed no longer has the arduous feel of "Nobody knows the trouble I've seen; nobody knows my sorrow." I've matured under the weight of the journey. I imagine it to be like the conditioning developed by an experienced mountain climber. And my perspective has changed so that my focus isn't on what I'm going *through*. It's on what I'm going *to*! The top of the mountain calls to me and draws me upward.

> Self-discipline moves you from good intentions to good actions.

My friend Jim Whittaker has climbed the great mountains of the world. One day at lunch he shared with me that his greatest accomplishment as a mountain climber was the number of people he had taken to the top with him. And he then gave me some climbing advice that I want to pass on to you. He said, "You never conquer the mountain. You only conquer yourself." That is the most important leadership journey each of us must make.

2. Self-Discipline Makes the Difference Between Temporary Success and Sustained Success

I want to add something important to my statement that everything worthwhile is uphill. Three words: *all the way*. Why is that significant? Anyone can climb for a short time. Nearly everyone does—at least once. But can you sustain it? Can you climb every day, day after day, year after year? I don't ask that to discourage you. I ask it because I want you to understand what it will take for you to reach your potential as a person and as a leader. That's why I say that the price tag of leadership is self-discipline.

Brian Tracy wrote about a chance encounter he had with legendary success author Kop Kopmeyer. When Tracy asked the author which was the most important of the thousands of success principles he'd discovered, Kopmeyer answered, "The most important success principle of all was stated by Thomas Huxley many years ago. He said, 'Do what you should do, when you should do it, whether you feel like it or not.'" Kopmeyer went on to say, "There are 999 other success principles that I have found in my reading and experience, but without self-discipline, none of them work."[3]

My friend Kevin Myers, pastor of 12Stone Church, says it this way: "Everyone is looking for a quick fix, but what they really need is fitness. People who seek fixes stop doing what's right as soon as the pressure they feel is relieved. People who pursue fitness do what they should no matter what the circumstances are."

> Do what you should do, when you should do it, whether you feel like it or not.
>
> —THOMAS HUXLEY

Every day we face the decision of whether we are going to pay the price tag of leadership. I like the way Rory Vaden looked at this issue in his book *Take the Stairs*. He called it the Pain Paradox. Are we going to do what's easy and *feels* good in the short term? Or are we going to do what's difficult and actually *is* good in the long term? Vadan said we ask ourselves:

> "Should I go ahead and buy that item or just save my money for a rainy day?"
> "Should I have that extravagant dessert or call it quits for the night?"
> "Should I put in the extra effort here or just get by with the minimum amount required?"[4]

These questions, Vaden said, reveal the Pain Paradox of decision making, which says:

> The short-term easy leads to the long-term difficult, while the short-term difficult leads to the long-term easy. The great paradox is that what we thought was the easy way, what looks like the easy way, what seems like the easy way very often leads us to creating a life that couldn't be

more opposite of easy. And inversely the things that we thought were most difficult, the challenges that appear to be the toughest, and the requirements that seem most rigorous are the very activities that lead us to the life of easy that we all want.[5]

> The short-term easy leads to the long-term difficult, while the short-term difficult leads to the long-term easy.
>
> —RORY VADEN

Vaden said the battle we fight is between our emotions, which typically have more power in the moment, and logic, which takes a longer view of life. That speaks to me because I have a sanguine personality, and it's very easy for me to live in the moment and to want to have fun. I discovered this early about myself, so I needed a strategy to help me focus on the long term and fight for future success. I wrote about my answer to that in my book *Today Matters*. I'll give you the gist of the idea here. I identified twelve major decision areas for my life based on my values, and I made a well-thought-out, logical decision for each of them. I call these decisions my Daily Dozen because my goal is to make my daily in-the-moment decisions based on these twelve values:

Just for today . . .   I will choose and display the right attitudes.
Just for today . . .   I will embrace and practice good values.
Just for today . . .   I will communicate with and care for my family.
Just for today . . .   I will know and follow healthy guidelines.
Just for today . . .   I will determine and act upon important priorities.
Just for today . . .   I will accept and show responsibility.
Just for today . . .   I will make and keep proper commitments.
Just for today . . .   I will initiate and invest in solid relationships.
Just for today . . .   I will earn and properly manage finances.
Just for today . . .   I will deepen and live out my faith.

Just for today . . .   I will desire and experience self-improvement.

Just for today . . .   I will plan for and model generosity.

Just for today . . .   I will act on these decisions and practice these disciplines.

Then one day . . .   I will see the compounding results of a day lived well.

When I feel the emotional pull to do what's not best for me, I choose to practice self-discipline by doing these twelve things that are right for me. If I do them with consistency, then someday success in those areas will show up for me. The emphasis here is on consistency, because consistency compounds.

3. Self-Discipline Makes Habit Your Servant Instead of Your Master

Every person has uphill hopes and aspirations. We all have uphill dreams. But we also have a problem. Every one of us also has downhill habits. And those are often what keep us from making the self-disciplined climb to higher ground. Why? Because habits have power over us. Take a look at this insightful piece written by Dennis P. Kimbro that I came across several years ago:

I am your constant companion.

I am your greatest helper or your heaviest burden.

I will push you onward or drag you down to failure.

I am completely at your command.

Half the things you do,

You might just as well turn over to me,

And I will be able to do them quickly and correctly.

I am easily managed—

You must merely be firm with me.

Show me exactly how you want something done,

And after a few lessons

I will do it automatically.

I am the servant of all great people.

And alas, of all failures as well.

Those who are great,

I have made great.

Those who are failures,

I have made failures.

I am not a machine,

Though I work with all the precision of a machine,

Plus, the intelligence of a human.

You may run me for profit, or run me for ruin.

It makes no difference to me.

Take me, train me, be firm with me,

And I will place the world at your feet.

Be easy with me, and I will destroy you.

Who am I?

I am a habit.[6]

The habits we have make us or break us. We choose which.

Every leader faces two challenges: First, how can I turn my downhill habits into uphill habits? Second, how can I help the people I lead to change their downhill habits into uphill ones? So the question is, how can we turn downhill habits into uphill habits that serve us instead of enslave us?

The first step in changing your habits is to change your thinking. If you can help others change their thinking, then you can help them change their habits too. What we think determines who we are. Who we are determines what we do. Bad thinking results in bad habits. Good thinking results in good habits. If I could do one thing for people, I would help them think in such a way that their choices would result in uphill habits.

Uphill thinking is deliberate, consistent, and willful. Downhill thinking is unintentional, inconsistent, and wishy-washy. Uphill thinking leads to uphill climbing. Downhill thinking leads to downhill sliding. Take a look at the difference:

Uphill Climbing	Downhill Sliding
Everything worthwhile	Nothing worthwhile
Wins	Losses
Preparing	Repairing
High morale	Low morale
High self-respect	Low self-respect
Self-improvement	No improvement
Purposeful	Aimless
Fulfilling	Empty
Making a difference	Not making a difference
Intentional actions (doing)	Good intentions (knowing)
Uphill habits	Downhill habits

Let me explain how this often plays out. If I have a problem or a challenge, and I think there is no positive solution, how will I respond? I'll probably procrastinate. Or I might start making excuses for why I won't take action. But excuses are exit signs that take us off the road of progress. Sometimes the results are tragic. Other times they're comical. For example, here are some excuses submitted in claims to auto insurance companies:

"As I reached the intersection, a hedge sprang up, obscuring my vision." (Don't you hate those instant hedges?)

"An invisible car came out of nowhere, struck my car, and vanished." (Like a superhero.)

"The telephone pole was approaching fast. I attempted to swerve out of its path when it struck my front end." (Those telephone poles have a mind of their own. They're so unpredictable.)

"The indirect cause of this accident was a little guy in a small car with a big mouth." (I can picture that one.)

"I had been driving my car for four years when I fell asleep at the wheel and had an accident." (That must be a record.)

"To avoid hitting the bumper of the car in front of me, I struck the pedestrian!" (That's an interesting choice.)

"I was on my way to the doctor's with rear-end trouble when my
universal joint gave way, causing me to have an accident." (I'm
not touching that one with a ten-foot pole!)

If my thinking is negative, I develop the habits of procrastination and
excuse making. But if my thinking is positive, I take responsibility and I
take action. My thinking determines my habits.

At the core of how we think is our overall attitude toward life. Many
people think life should be easy. That thinking causes them to expect
everything to come to them without effort. They watch and wait, hoping
success will come and find them. It won't. We can settle and assume that
everything will come to us. Or we can take control of our lives and make
things happen. If we don't take control of our lives, someone else will.
And they may not want what we want for our lives.

Dan Cathy, chairman and CEO of Chick-fil-A, recently shared
with me that the rate of internal change must be faster than the rate
of external change. That's the right way to think of it. Keep growing
and changing on the inside, starting with your thinking, because self-
discipline in the area of thinking will help you change from downhill
habits to uphill hopes. The old wisdom is true: For as he thinks within
himself, so he is.[7]

4. SELF-DISCIPLINE IS DEVELOPED—NOT GIVEN

One of my favorite golf courses is at the Highlands Country Club in
Highlands, North Carolina. It is the golf course that Bobby Jones played
on for many years. In fact, he opened
the fairways by hitting the first ball off
the tee there in 1928.

> Self-discipline in the area of thinking will help you change from downhill habits to uphill hopes.

Bobby Jones was a golf prodigy
who went on to become a legend.
He began playing in 1907 at age
five. By age twelve, he was scoring
below par, an accomplishment most golfers don't achieve in a lifetime
of playing the game. At fourteen he qualified for the US Amateur

Championship. But Jones didn't win that event. His problem can be best described by the nickname he acquired: "club thrower." Jones often lost his temper—and his ability to play well. And his temper was the thing that kept him from his true golf potential, not anything related to his skill. Poor self-discipline had the potential to be his downfall.

An old golfer whom Jones called Grandpa Bart had given up the game because of arthritis, but he still worked part-time in the pro shop. One day he told Jones, "Bobby, you are good enough to win that tournament, but you'll never win until you can control that temper of yours. You miss a shot—you get upset—and then you lose."

Jones listened to the older man's advice and began working to discipline his emotions. At age twenty-one, Jones blossomed and went on to be one of the greatest golfers in history. He retired after winning the grand slam of golf. He was only twenty-eight. Grandpa Bart's comment said it all: "Bobby was fourteen when he mastered the game of golf, but he was twenty-one when he mastered himself."

Lack of discipline is the lid on many people's potential. That's the bad news. However, there's also good news: self-discipline is not something you have to be born with. It is something you can develop. It's earned, not given. In other words, if the lack of self-discipline has been a lid for you, as it was for Bobby Jones, you can remove that lid. It is within your power.

The first step to developing self-discipline is awareness. You need to see where you're falling short. Jones was fortunate that someone was willing to speak into his life and point out his problem. Not all of us are so lucky. We may need to seek out people who know us and are willing to tell us the truth.

I want to give you three tips to help you develop self-discipline if this has been a difficult area for you.

Self-Disciplined People Avoid Temptation

Recently, during a time I was working hard to lose weight, my friend Traci Morrow, who was coaching me, said, "John, the success of your diet is determined at the grocery store. Don't bring home food that is not good for you. Leave it on the shelves of the store, not on the shelves in your kitchen."

People who develop self-discipline and positive habits don't put themselves in the line of fire. If they want to lose weight, they don't keep junk food in their desk drawers. If they're trying to stop spending money, they don't go hang out at the mall. They *intentionally* avoid temptation.

Self-Disciplined People Know When to Expend Their Energy

It is impossible to be at 100 percent all day, every day. And it's not necessary. Knowing when to be at 100 percent is essential to self-discipline. Why? Because you only have a certain amount of energy. You need to choose when to use it.

Every day I look at my calendar and ask myself, "When do I need to be at my best?" After identifying those times, I then monitor my energy and effort to get the most out of myself during those crucial moments. I apply the energy required for me to practice self-discipline at those times when I need it the most.

Gary Keller, founder of Keller Williams Realty, said, "Make sure every day you . . . know what matters most."[8] That's great advice. Think ahead and match up your energy to the things that matter most.

Self-Disciplined People Understand and Practice the Principle of Pay Now, Play Later

There are two types of people in the area of discipline. One type puts off what needs to be done and plays now, preferring to avoid doing what he or she must. The other type pays now by doing the necessary, even if it's unpleasant, and is willing to defer fun and play later. The thing you need to know is that everybody pays. Whatever you put off until later always compounds. If you put off playing,

> Make sure every day you . . . know what matters most.
>
> —GARY KELLER

you get to play more later. If you put off paying, you have to pay more later. There is no cheating in life.

Intuitively, you know this is true. If you pay into your retirement funds and invest early in life, you have more money available to you in your older years. If you spend it all while you're young, you won't be able to play in your old age. If you pay by eating right and exercising throughout your early life, your health will be better as you grow old. If you neglect those things, you'll pay for it as you age. It's your choice.

Recently I shared with a group of students, "If you only do what you want to do, you will never get to do what you really want to do." Self-discipline is developed by saying yes when we want to say no and saying no when we want to say yes. There are two types of pain in life: the pain of self-discipline, which is eased by doing the right thing, and the pain of regret, which aches until we die.

5. SELF-DISCIPLINE IS MOST EASILY DEVELOPED IN AREAS OF STRENGTH AND PASSION

German playwright Carl Zuckmayer said, "One half of life is luck; the other half is discipline, and that's the important half. For without discipline you wouldn't know what to do with luck." Where do you find the discipline that leads to success? By doing the *right* thing every day. That right thing usually involves your strengths and your passion. What you love and what you're good at usually point you to your right thing.

Self-discipline always needs fuel. The strongest fuel comes from inspiration and motivation, which are usually connected with your strengths. What you do well usually inspires you and others. And motivation is a by-product of your passion. If you love to do something, you're almost always motivated to do it.

If you are focusing on developing your self-discipline in the areas of your strengths and passion, the race of life feels easier to run, and you run it faster. If you are trying to develop discipline in areas where you are not gifted or passionate, the race feels long and arduous. Discipline fueled by your strengths and passion is easier to convert into positive habits too. And even though you may not be great at anything you do for the first time, if the task is connected to your giftedness or passion, you will learn to do it well quickly and with a higher degree of skill.

For years I have spent most of my time developing self-discipline in the areas of my strengths because they complement my purpose. When I'm working within my *why*, my reason for being on this planet, I am able to remain motivated long after the first rush of enthusiasm and excited energy wears off. I guess you could call it *why power*. It can carry you forward when willpower is not enough.

If the time, energy, and resources of your life are focused on areas not related to your strengths or passion, I want to encourage you to rethink what you're doing. Maybe it's time to

- Quit something you don't do well to do something you do well.
- Quit something you're not passionate about to do something that fills you with passion.
- Quit something that doesn't make a difference to do something that does.
- Quit something that's not your dream to do something that is.

If you change what you do, will it always be pleasant or easy? No. But everyone should say no to the good so they can say yes to the best.

6. SELF-DISCIPLINE AND RESPECT ARE CONNECTED

Few things build self-respect the way self-discipline does. Author and speaker Brian Tracy said, "Disciplining yourself to do what you know is right and important, although difficult, is the high road to pride, self-esteem, and personal satisfaction."

Respect is the fruit of the disciplined life, both self-respect and the respect of others. When talking about developing relationships with others, I've often said that respect is earned on difficult ground. But we also earn self-respect on difficult ground. Self-discipline is its own reward.

Discipline-Driven People	Emotion-Driven People
Do right, then feel good	Feel good, then do right
Are commitment-driven	Are convenience-driven
Make principle-based decisions	Make popular-based decisions
Action controls attitude	Attitude controls action
Believe it, then see it	See it, then believe it
Create momentum	Wait for momentum
Ask, "What are my responsibilities?"	Ask, "What are my rights?"
Continue when problems arise	Quit when problems arise
Are steady	Are moody
Can be leaders	Will be followers

The late Louis L'Amour is one of the bestselling authors of all time. More than 900 million copies of his books have been sold worldwide, and even though he died in 1988, every one of his books is still in print.[9] When asked the key to his writing style, he responded, "Start writing, no matter what. The water does not flow until the faucet is turned on." Turning the faucet on is the beginning. Respect is a result of keeping it on. Self-discipline allows you to do that.

We earn self-respect on difficult ground.

7. SELF-DISCIPLINE MAKES CONSISTENCY POSSIBLE, AND CONSISTENCY COMPOUNDS

Consistency is not a sexy word. Why? Consistency doesn't prove itself quickly, and it isn't rewarded immediately. In today's culture, people are more captivated by charisma, genius, excitement, creativity, and innovation. But I can tell you after fifty years of striving for consistency, the dividends can be extraordinary. Here are just a few of the things consistency can do for you:

Consistency Establishes Your Reputation

Anybody can be good once in a while. Only the self-disciplined are consistently good. And that consistency makes people notice you—and expect you to deliver. On August 6, 1999, I traveled with my son-in-law, Steve Miller, to Montreal, Canada, because of the reputation of someone who consistently delivered. His name was Tony Gwynn, an outfielder for the San Diego Padres. One of the greatest hitters ever to play major league baseball, Gwynn was on the verge of getting his 3,000th hit against the Expos. Only thirty players in the history of professional baseball have ever accomplished that feat.[10] Nearly all of them are in the Hall of Fame. How did Tony accomplish this? One hit at a time, game after game, year after year.

Consistency Is a Prerequisite to Excellence

Anytime you try something for the first time, you won't be any good at it. That's just the way it is. So why try anything new? Because we all have to start somewhere. The first step is to master the basics. But then what? You don't just jump to excellence. The road to get there is consistency. Improvement is possible only through consistent practice.

Consistency Provides Security to Others

As leaders, one of the things we can provide to the people we lead is a sense of stability. Perhaps the highest compliment we can ever receive as leaders are the words, "I can depend on you." When people see your consistency and know they can rely on you, it gives them a sense of security.

Consistency Reinforces Your Vision and Values

Effective leadership is highly visual. Why? People do what people see. Leaders are models of behavior for those they lead. When team members see their leader doing something, they often follow in their footsteps—for good or ill. The leader cuts corners, they cut corners. The leader shows up late, they show up late. The leader performs only when he or she feels like it, they perform only when they feel like it. However, when the leader pays the price, shows up early, keeps promises, and delivers the goods *consistently*, then most of the people on the team strive to do likewise.

Consistency Compounds

I started speaking publicly in 1968. I made a commitment to train leaders in 1976. I started writing books in 1979. And I began developing and creating resources in 1984. Each time I added another leadership objective, I didn't neglect the previous one. I kept working at it. I now look back and am surprised by what I've accomplished. I've spoken more than twelve thousand times. My organizations have trained more than 5 million leaders from every country of the world. I've produced more than one hundred books. My success has come because I started young, I've worked consistently, and I'm now seventy. That's the compounding potential of consistency.

I can remember times when I was tempted to take shortcuts. When I was twenty-three, I realized that I could wing it speaking instead of putting in the hard work of preparation before I addressed an audience. I could have gotten away with taking this easy road. I *wanted* to take this easy road, because it would have given me more time to do other things I wanted to do. But I knew deep down that it would be a mistake. If I relied on the talent I had to get me through, I would not be able to build on that talent and improve. So I did the work. That decision has paid off time after time over the years.

Successful people do daily what unsuccessful people do only occasionally. The bookends of success are beginning well and ending well. What is between those bookends? Consistency. If you want to become the leader you have the *potential* to be, you need to pay the price of self-discipline.

One last word about self-discipline before we move on to the last chapter: most of the good leaders I know have a strong desire to help others. They want to invest in their team members, they want to grow their organizations, and they want to lead others to do something significant. You probably feel those desires too. You may have a strong pull to make a difference in this world. If so, there's something you need to know. Leaders are

> Successful people do daily what unsuccessful people do only occasionally.

responsible to help themselves and make themselves better before they try to help others.

If you've ever flown on an airplane, you've heard the safety instructions from the flight attendants. What do they say? Put the oxygen mask on yourself before you put it on your child or someone who may need your assistance. Why? Because it is impossible to help others effectively until you have first helped yourself. Self-discipline is what enables you to do that. If there's one thing to fight for as a leader, this is it, because it unlocks the door to so many other abilities: character, priorities, influence, and serving people. If you win the battles within, all the other victories become within reach.

DEVELOPING THE *SELF-DISCIPLINED* PERSON WITHIN YOU

Self-discipline is not something you fight for once and say, "Whew, I'm glad that's over." It's something you need to keep working for day after day. But here's the good news: the more self-discipline battles you've won, the less difficult the subsequent battles usually are. One victory builds upon another, and each discipline you do practice helps you with the others you desire to do.

Start Somewhere—Get Wins Under Your Belt

As I mentioned in the chapter, self-discipline isn't given. It must be developed by every individual who possesses it. If discipline is something you have neglected or struggled with in the past, you need to set yourself up for success with small victories. Try beginning in these areas:

- *Avoid Temptation:* In what area of your life can you draw the line of safety far away from the point of temptation? Traci coached me not to buy junk food when I was at the store so I wouldn't be tempted to eat the wrong foods at home. Where can you draw the line?

- **Pay Now, Play Later:** Pick small, winnable tasks that you can do *before* rewarding yourself with fun or relaxation. Anytime you can delay gratification and practice self-discipline, you've won. Let yourself feel good about it, and use it to help you *want* to practice self-discipline.

- **Get Back on the Wagon:** We all fail, and that can be discouraging. Don't allow a mistake or a lapse in discipline to make you give up. Acknowledge the failure, learn from it, identify temptations to avoid, and get back on the self-discipline wagon.

DEVELOP DISCIPLINE IN YOUR STRENGTHS

While you're creating or strengthening a strong foundation of discipline in your life, start building upon your strengths. What do you do well? What are your talents? What are you passionate about? How can you leverage these things for your life and your leadership?

Pick one area of your life where winning comes more easily, and identify one discipline you could practice to strengthen that area. Plan it, schedule it, and do follow-through *consistently*.

TEN

THE EXPANSION OF LEADERSHIP:
PERSONAL GROWTH

On my fortieth birthday I wrote a lesson titled "I'm 40 and Counting." It was a reflective lesson where I examined my life, assessed how I had done some things poorly and some well, and taught the ten things I believed all people should try to get under their belts by age forty. Writing the lesson was so fulfilling and the response was so positive that when I turned fifty, I did a lesson called "I'm 50 and Reflecting: The Most Important Lessons I've Learned in My Life." When I turned sixty . . . You can see where this is going! I'll just cut to the chase. I've written two other lessons: "I'm 60 and Compounding" and "I'm 70 and Transforming." If I live to be eighty, you know what I'll be doing for my birthday.

Those lessons have been markers in my life. Looking back over the decades, I think I have a better handle on what really matters. I'm certain of fewer things now at seventy than I was at forty, but I'm more certain of those few things than I've ever been in my life. One of those things—and it's been my biggest takeaway from writing those lessons—is that growth matters. My capacity to grow has determined my capacity to lead. Today I lead differently and more effectively than I did at forty. And it's not just because I've been leading longer. It's been because I've made personal growth a priority all these years.

At one of my conferences several years ago, a man about my age approached me during a break and said, "I wish I would have heard you twenty years ago."

"No, you don't," I answered.

"You don't understand," he responded. "I said I wish I had heard you twenty years ago."

"You really don't," I said.

Now he was starting to get frustrated. "If I would have heard what you said today, twenty years ago, it would have changed my life."

"But that's the problem," I replied. "Twenty years ago I couldn't have taught you what you learned today. I hadn't learned it yet back then." His expression changed from frustration to understanding, and he laughed. We both did.

I love to talk and write about personal growth. It's one of my passions. I have seen firsthand how effectively a life committed to continual personal growth produces results beyond our wildest imaginings. Because I've seen the power of growth, I'm always fired up to share the principles and practices that will help people make it a habit. That's the how-to of growth. But before anyone is ready to learn the *how* of growth, they need to embrace the *why*.

GROWTH MATTERS

Your capacity to grow will determine your capacity to lead. Growth matters. If you try to lead out of what you learned long in the past, and you're not growing in the present, the clock is ticking on your time as a leader. Development, expansion, and the future of your leadership depend on your dedication to personal growth. Here's why I say this:

1. Growth Is the Only Guarantee That Tomorrow Will Get Better

In July 2015 I went to my fiftieth high school reunion in Circleville, Ohio. I had not seen most of my high school classmates since I graduated, so I was excited to renew relationships with people after so many years. I pictured the faces of the friends I looked forward to seeing.

My wife, Margaret, and I arrived late to the party. As we walked into the main room, I looked around and stopped. Was I in the wrong place?

"Margaret, there are a lot of old people here!" I said. She laughed.

"John, maybe you need to look in the mirror," was all she said.

That night I enjoyed catching up with my classmates and taking pictures with them. However, by the end of that evening, I felt slightly depressed. For three hours I had listened to people talk about themselves, the good old days, and the medicines they were taking. *Is this what we've come to?* I thought. By the time we got to our rental car, I was feeling old too.

The passing of time guarantees that we will get older, but it doesn't guarantee we will get better. I know I'm getting older, but I'm not giving in to my age. I want my future to get better. That requires continual personal growth. That evening at our hotel, I sat down and wrote the following:

Five Ways to Intentionally Not Act Old

1. **Ask Questions:** Old people aren't inquisitive. When you stop asking questions, you have lost interest in life. I will remain inquisitive.
2. **Keep the Bar of Excellence High:** Old people lower their standards. They get tired and complacent. I will raise the bar.
3. **Be People-Centric:** Old people become self-absorbed. They talk about themselves, their ailments, and their medications. I will focus on others.
4. **Be Posture-Conscious:** Old people slouch. You look younger when you stand tall. I will work on my posture.
5. **Remain Today-Focused:** Old people talk about yesterday. I will look forward and talk about today.

That same weekend, I went out to eat with my high school basketball teammates. We had a great meal and told old stories about our basketball team. The longer we talked, the better players we were. We talked about our shooting prowess, our fast-break offense, our crushing defense. We concluded that we were a really good team.

Then Tom Smith said, "Guys, I brought video of one of our games."

"Let's watch it!" we all agreed, pumping our fists and high-fiving each other.

Tom cued it up. In seconds reality set in. Where was the speed we'd talked about? Somebody asked, "Is the video in slow motion?"

"No," Smitty said.

I watched my seventeen-year-old self throw up a bad shot. We botched plays. We turned over the ball. We took dumb shots, which we missed. Our defense fell apart. None of what we were seeing on video matched the greatness of the play we had remembered. Midway through the first quarter, John Thomas stood up and said, "I'm going to get some dessert." The rest of us followed him. That night we realized that the good old days weren't really that good. And if there was a silver lining in that experience, it's this: the fact that yesterday didn't look very good to us was an indication that we had grown.

There are many good reasons to pursue personal growth. It opens doors. It makes us better. It helps us achieve our career goals. Over time, it creates momentum in our lives. That in turn encourages us to grow even more. We start to place a greater emphasis on growing than on arriving, and that makes it easier for us to learn from our failure. But all of those things pale against the most important reason to pursue growth, because this reason has the greatest power to change our lives in every way. Personal growth increases hope. It teaches us that tomorrow can be better than today. Here's how.

> Personal growth increases hope. It teaches us that tomorrow can be better than today.

A Growth Mind-Set Is the Seed of Hope

Think about the world of nature. A sapling becomes a mighty oak by growing slowly over time. An infant grows into a child, who eventually becomes an adult. Hope is the same way. It looks forward. When we have hope, we can imagine a better future. And hope isn't just wishing for things that might be. It's the firm belief in things that will be. It's looking past your present circumstances with the belief that you have a positive future.

Planting the seed of growth is not complicated. It's as simple as a change in mind-set. When we decide to believe that growth is possible and we commit to pursuing it, hope begins to rise within us. The change in focus is only the first step, but it can be the beginning of a long and rewarding journey.

A Growth Habit Strengthens Hope

Choosing to grow is important, but that decision is not enough to create change on its own. We need to acknowledge that growth is a gradual process and make that process part of our daily practice. That means we need to establish the *habit* of growing on a consistent basis.

When you practice the discipline of growing a little every day, you are doing your part to strengthen the hope inside of you. With each small step you take, you make progress toward improving yourself and your world. It's like humorist Garrison Keillor once said, "There's only so much you can do, but you must do that much—even if you don't know how much that is." When you grow, you are putting your future into motion. And with every step toward the future, hope is reinforced and strengthened. That process becomes sustainable when you make growth a habit.

Growth Sustained over Time Realizes Hope

Growth over time helps us to live out our hope. When we take small steps of growth every day, over time, we see progress. If you string together enough days of consistent growth, you begin to change as a person. You become better, stronger, more skilled, or all of the above. And when you change yourself, you can change your circumstances. This begins a positive cycle of your growth strengthening your hope, and your hope strengthening your growth. When you do this week after week, month after month, year after year, you gradually move from hope imagined to hope realized.

2. Growth Means Change

During a break at a conference where I was teaching, a young man came up to me and said, "I'd like to do what you do." I'm sure it looked appealing. He was part of a great audience of two thousand people who were eager to learn. Thanks to my staff, the conference was running smoothly, and people flooded the lobby, buying books and coming up to me to get them signed. I think he could imagine himself onstage, delivering a message to a large, appreciative audience.

"Of course," I said. "Who wouldn't enjoy all this?" I looked around the auditorium, trying to capture everything around us. "But I have a question for you," I continued. "Would you like to do what I did so you can do what I do?"

His expression changed. I don't think it had occurred to him that I had taken a very long and sometimes painful journey to get to where I was.

That's common with all of us. We see star athletes or talented musicians at the top of their game, and we don't understand the sacrifice and hard work it took for them to get there. Only the person who had the dream and took the journey truly knows what it required. The cost of change is often the great separator between those who grow and those who do not, between those who grow into their dreams and those who dream but remain where they are.

For years I wanted to write a book that would help people realize their dreams, but I didn't want the book to be hollow inspiration. I wanted to be encouraging, but I wanted to help people build their future on reality, not fluffy aspirations. It took me awhile to figure out the right approach, but I finally was able to write a book called *Put Your Dream to the Test*. It contains ten questions you must ask and answer to determine if your dream can become a reality.

Of those ten questions, one question stands above all others in determining the possibility of achieving the dream. It's the Cost Question: Am I willing to pay the price for my dream? Sometimes I think I should have tweaked the Cost Question to say, "Am I willing to *continually* pay the price for my dream?" As my friend Gerald Brooks often says, "Every level of growth calls for a new level of change." It also calls for more from you. I've discovered that the price of change usually comes sooner than you think, it's higher than you imagined it would be, and it must be paid more often than you expected. In fact, to continue growing is to continue paying the price of that growth.

Life begins at the end of our comfort zone. To grow, we must embrace change and learn to become comfortable being uncomfortable. The comfort zone is characterized by doing the same things in the same ways with the same people at the same time and getting the same results. People remain in their comfort zones yet ask why their lives don't get any better. That's crazy. Doing the same thing every day will not help you succeed. Growth always requires change.

> Every level of growth calls for a new level of change.
>
> —GERALD BROOKS

The Law of the Rubber Band in *The 15 Invaluable Laws of Growth* says that growth stops when you lose the tension between where you are and where you should be.[1] What makes any rubber band useful? Stretching. There is no practical use for a rubber band unless it has been stretched. The same can be said of us. Social commentator and philosopher Eric Hoffer said, "In a time of drastic change it is the learners who inherit the future. The learned usually find themselves equipped to live in a world that no longer exists."[2]

That could have been a description of the world I found myself in during the early years of my leadership. The organization I was connected with resisted change and therefore forfeited much of its growth potential. (Their idea of progress was to move backward slowly.) I felt torn between the people I loved who wanted me to stay the same as I was and the new growth I was experiencing that made me desire to change and take risks to reach my potential. After months of internal emotional wrestling, I decided that I would follow the path of personal growth. The words of author Gail Sheehy describe my thinking:

If we don't change, we don't grow. If we don't grow, we are not really living. Growth demands a temporary surrender of security. It may mean a giving up of familiar but limiting patterns, safe but unrewarding work, values no longer believed in, relationships that have lost their meaning. As Dostoyevsky put it, 'taking a new step, uttering a new word, is what people fear most.' The real fear should be the opposite course.[3]

The process I went through was challenging at first. It had its ups and downs. Any progress I made in my growth revealed how much more I had to learn. Psychologist Herbert Gerjuoy said, "The illiterate of the future are not those who cannot read or write, but those who cannot learn, unlearn and relearn."[4] That's what I had to keep doing: learning, unlearning, and relearning. Change became constant because each new challenge and each new level of growth required a better and different me.

I can give you an illustration of this in how I learned to become a better writer. In 1977 my mentor, author Les Parrott Jr., shared with me that if I wanted to influence people beyond my personal reach, I should start to write books. The day he spoke those words to me was the day I decided to become a writer. The decision was instant, but the process of learning to write well was long and arduous. To accomplish this, I followed the learn, unlearn, relearn process:

Learn: "What do I need to learn today that I didn't know yesterday?"

I immersed myself in the world of writing. I took classes on writing. I interviewed writers. I asked authors to mentor me. I read books, studied their style, and developed a style that seemed to fit me. And I wrote consistently. In ten years I wrote seven books. They all had one thing in common: they didn't sell well.

Unlearn: "What do I need to let go of today that I held on to yesterday?"

Before I decided to write books, all my writing had been for my speaking. I had to learn a different set of skills. I had to separate my speaking from my writing. Speaking was easy for me, and I was effective even at a young age. I had learned how to use my voice to command attention and make the most of my persona and charisma. I had learned how to read a crowd and connect with them. None of those skills carried over into my book writing.

Relearn: "What do I need to change today that I was doing yesterday?"

I had to develop writing connections to the reader. I had to learn how to think the way a reader thought and anticipate people's responses at my desk instead of onstage. That was difficult. As I worked hard to discover and develop a new way of writing, I would continually ask myself, "Will the reader turn the page?" After years of hard work and many changes, I can say with confidence that I have learned to connect with the reader.

The growth journey from here to there is often lonely because you have to be willing to be wrong and you have to be willing to change. Growth comes as the result of dropping bad habits, changing wrong priorities, and embracing new ways of thinking. The people who do not grow get stuck because they are unwilling to leave what they have known and practiced to do something better. They are not willing to risk being wrong so they can discover what is right. Ironically, they cling to the right, but their lives turn out wrong.

If you want to grow as a person and as a leader, you must be willing to surrender feeling right so that you can find what actually is right. Doing this doesn't require you to be brilliant, talented, or lucky. It just means you have to be willing to change and be uncomfortable.

3. GROWTH IS THE GREAT SEPARATOR BETWEEN THOSE WHO SUCCEED AND THOSE WHO DON'T

If you have a desire to be successful, you cannot allow yourself to settle for being average. Why? Have you ever gotten *excited* about eating at an average restaurant? Have you ever gushed to others about an average vacation? Do you find deep fulfillment in an average relationship? Do you heartily recommend an average movie to friends? Of course not. Average is never good enough. You must strive for excellence.

Recently I came across a piece by telecommunications executive team leader David Lewis that describes what it means to be average:

"Average" is what failures claim to be when their friends ask them
why they are not more successful.

"Average" is the top of the bottom, the best of the worst, the
bottom of the top, the worst of the top. Which of these are you?

"Average" means being run-of-the-mill, mediocre, insignificant, an
also-ran, a non-entity.

Being "average" is the lazy person's cop-out; it's lacking guts to take
a stand in life; it's living by default.

Being "average" is to take up space for no purpose; to take a train
through life but never to pay the fare; to return no interest for
God's investment in you.

Being "average" is to pass one's life away with time, rather than
to pass one's time away with life; it's to kill time, rather than
working it to death.

To be "average" is to be forgotten once you pass from this life. The
successful are remembered for their contributions; the failures
are remembered because they tried; but the "average," the silent
majority, are just forgotten.

To be "Average" is to commit the greatest crime one can against
oneself, humanity, and one's God. The saddest epitaph is this:
"Here lies Mr. and Mrs. Average—here lie the remains of
what might have been, except for their belief that they were
"average."[5]

Are these thoughts a little harsh? Maybe. But if they stir you up and
inspire you to get out of your comfort zone, then they have achieved a
noble purpose. It's okay to be content with what you have, but it's never
okay to be so content with who you are that you stop growing.

Growth's highest reward is not what
we get from it, but what we become
because of it. I made personal growth my
goal the day I learned that growth was
not automatic, that we don't grow just by
living. The beginning of my growth journey was marked by many goals. However,

> Growth's highest reward is not
> what we get from it, but what
> we become because of it.

Goal Conscious	Growth Conscious
Focus is on a destination	Focus is on the journey
Motivates people	Matures people
Goals are seasonal	Growth is lifelong
Challenges people	Changes people
When the goal is reached, we stop	When the goal is reached, we keep growing
Goal Question: How long will this take?	Growth Question: How far can I go?

as I matured and changed because of growth, I became less enamored with goals and more passionate about growth. The result? Today I am consistently growth conscious. Here is the difference.

I like to tell people I'm a mountain climber. People who know me well look at me funny. My body doesn't look like it has climbed any mountains. Before they can say anything, I tell them, "The mountain I climb is called Growth." Every day I take a few steps up toward my potential. Even at seventy, I'm still climbing. The result?

> The Law of Diminishing Intent says that the longer you wait to do something you should do now, the greater the odds that you will never do it.

I've outgrown yesterday and grown into tomorrow.
I've outgrown old expectations and grown into new expectations.
I've outgrown past victories and grown into present victories.
I've outgrown average relationships and grown into improving relationships.
I've outgrown what was and grown into what could be.
I've outgrown success and grown into significance.

I hope you are getting the picture of what growth can do for you. I hope the desire to grow is starting to burn brightly within you. The Law of Diminishing Intent says that the longer you wait to do something you should do now, the greater the odds that you will never do it.[6] If you haven't already begun the journey, start climbing today. Come join me as we move forward for the mountaintop and make the slow but steady climb far beyond average.

4. For Growth to Be Maximized, It Must Be Strategic

The biggest and most important project you will ever take on is your own life. Unfortunately, most people plan their vacations better than they plan their lives. But as author and speaker Jim Rohn said, "If you don't design your own life plan, chances are you'll fall into someone else's plan. And guess what they may have planned for you? Not much!" For that reason, you need to be intentional and strategic.

Michael Gerber, author of The E-Myth, said, "Systems permit ordinary people to achieve extraordinary results." Strategies are nothing more than systems for obtaining specific results. I think of systems as being like freeways. They get me where I want to go quickly and efficiently. In the span of a few years, I went from "What is a growth plan?" to "I have a plan, here's how it works, and here's what it's doing for me." That's the power of having strategic systems.

As you develop your strategies for personal growth, make sure they include these four elements:

The Big Picture—Where Do I Need to Focus My Growth?

My growth plan in the beginning could be summed up in one word: grow. That's not very specific, but that's where I started. The good news is that as I grew, so did my awareness of the picture for my leadership. Questions began to surface in my mind. In what areas should I try to grow? What resources do I need? Where can I get them? How much time should I spend on each area of growth? What mentors should I pursue? What experiences do I need to help me grow? Each question expanded my growth picture. The more I have grown, the greater my picture of growth has become.

Early on I learned that activity is not necessarily accomplishment. I needed to focus. I began to prioritize what I did and when I did it. For example, I'm a morning person. That's my best time for thinking and doing, so I began putting my most important growth projects in the early morning. My best time was given to my most important growth priorities.

I also started to refine what I did to grow and how I did it. I began to focus on three main areas:

- **My strengths—the areas of giftedness that set me apart from average.** Growing in my strengths enables me to reach the top 10 percent of people with a certain skill set. Almost all success is a result of being in the top 10 percent of a certain area. If you are in the top 20 percent, others will notice and admire you. If you're in the top 10 percent, people will seek you out and follow you.
- **My choices—the areas of weakness that need to change for my overall improvement.** Making the right choices is the fastest way to grow because you are in control of your choices. Improvement in this area adds value to your strengths. I wrote a book titled *Talent Is Never Enough*. I still believe that idea is true, but I also believe that talent plus good choices is more than enough to make you successful.
- **My faith—my relationship with God that influences my relationships with others.** My faith is foundational to everything I am and everything I do. Growth in this area enhances my life and the lives of those I influence.

What constitutes your big picture? Where do you want to go? What are the strengths you can develop? What choices can you make in foundational areas that will improve you? What core values do you need to include in your growth process? If you can answer these questions now, they will help you be more strategic in your personal growth. However, you may be like I was when I first got started—I didn't know what I didn't know. I had to start the growth process to begin seeing the big picture. If that describes you, then start where you are, allow the big picture to unfold, and make adjustments to your growth priorities as the picture becomes clearer.

Measurement—How Can I Measure and Affect My Growth?

What gets measured gets done. How will you know what progress you're making until you find some way to track your growth? I have to say, it's important to do, but it's also difficult. It requires evaluation and reflection.

I've found that it's easier to track progress periodically rather than to try to gauge it daily, because trying to assess your own growth that frequently is like trying to detect if children are growing. When you see your own children every day, you can't tell they've grown. But if you didn't see them for three months or a year, the changes would stand out.

I do my major growth measurement at the end of every year. At that time I spend time reflecting and going back through my calendar for the year, and I ask myself two questions: "Who stretched me?" and "What stretched me?"

As I think about the first question, I list the names of people who were catalysts for growth in my life. I try to figure out how I can spend more time with them in the coming year. I also write down the names of people who take my time but there's no value for either of us in the relationship. I figure out how to spend less time with them.

As I'm looking over the calendar for the past year, I think about the second question. To determine which ideas, experiences, events, stories, resources, and thoughts enlarged me. I use my answers to evaluate past experiences, target future ones, and start planning key growth experiences for the coming year. In my early years of growth, everyone and everything stretched me. As I've grown and experienced more, I've had to become more intentional and selective about how I spend my growth time. But the intention is always the same. I want to be *stretched*. Here's why:

- Once a mind is stretched, it cannot return to its original dimensions.
- Once a heart is stretched, it cannot return to its original dimensions.
- Once an idea is stretched, it cannot return to its original dimensions.

- Once hope is stretched, it cannot return to its original dimensions.
- Once passion is stretched, it cannot return to its original dimensions.
- Once work is stretched, it cannot return to its original dimensions.
- Once a team is stretched, it cannot return to its original dimensions.

Once you've grown, you will be forever impacted. And if you can see your progress, you'll never want to stop growing. A butterfly cannot go back to being a caterpillar. After forty-five years of intentional growing, I cannot go back. I have no desire to. Neither will you.

Consistency—How Can I Grow Daily?

For years I have taught that the secret of a person's success is determined by what he or she does daily. I recently heard former first lady Laura Bush say, "All we have is now." Wow! That's simple but profound. There will never be another now. Taking care of today and every day will ensure that someday your *now* will turn into *wow*.

I am intentional in my pursuit of growth by doing certain things every day:

> The secret of a person's success is determined by what he or she does daily.

- *I Make Growth My Number One Priority.* A day without growth is not acceptable to me. I am conscious of my need to learn twenty-four hours a day, seven days a week.
- *I Look for Growth Opportunities in Every Situation.* I know opportunities are there, so I actively look for them. I ask myself, "Do I see an opportunity? And have I taken advantage of it?"
- *I Ask Questions That Will Help Me Grow.* Growth doesn't come looking for me. I must proactively find it. I seek growth by continually asking questions.

- *I File What I Learn Every Day.* The number-one time waster is looking for things that are lost. I file ideas, quotes, and stories so I can find them quickly.
- *I Pass On to Others What I'm Learning.* I'm *always* thinking about sharing what I discover because it reinforces learning. It also adds value to the people to whom I pass it along.

What must you do to ensure that you're learning and growing every day? Use my list or create your own. Just be sure to make growth something you do *every* day, not *some*day.

Application—Can I Act on It?

Knowledge doesn't make a person better. Application does. Anything that doesn't get put into action remains theoretical. But the goal of personal growth is to become better—to become better as a person, a parent, a spouse, an employee, an employer, or a leader. We can experience change and still be passive. But to experience growth, we must be active.

We have to take control of our personal growth, accept responsibility for it, and do something with it. While others may lead small lives, we cannot. While others see themselves as victims, we will not. While others will leave their future in someone else's hands, we will not. While others simply *go* through life, I will *grow* through life. Make that choice, and do not surrender.

Whenever I'm writing a book or a lesson, I ask myself, "Can people receive this? Can they reproduce what I do? Can they apply it? Will it help them?" Why do I ask myself these questions? Because application stimulates transformation. Nothing happens with information unless it is applied. Every time I learn something, I ask myself, "Where can I use this? When can I use this? Who needs to know this?" The sooner I ask those questions and act on them, the greater the return for me and others.

5. Growth Is Joy

When I was in my thirties, one of my mentors told me, "Growth is happiness." That statement really stuck with me, and for many years I repeated it. But my perspective on that has changed, and today my appreciation for growth has deepened. For me, growth is more than just happiness. It's joy.

Why do I say that? First, growth has filled my life. It's made me bigger on the inside than I am on the outside. Most people at my age are worn down by work. Instead, because I've been filling my well with thoughts, ideas, experiences, and changes that have grown me for more than fifty years, I don't feel worn out. I feel as if I'm just warmed up.

Second, I'm living my mission and passion, which is to add value to leaders who multiply value to others. I get to live my passion every day, and my growth is targeted to help me fulfill my mission better.

Author Napoleon Hill said, "It's not what you are going to do, but it's what you are doing right now that counts." Every day for forty-five years, I've focused my "right now" on my mission. It's the most rewarding thing I can do. It gives me great joy. And I'm able to do it only because I've made growth my constant companion. Entertainer Dolly Parton said, "Find out who you really are and do it on purpose."[7] That's what I've done. And I continue to take joy in it. Why? Because it aligns with who I am:

I want to keep making a difference.
I never want to stop growing.
I want to use my best gifts.
I feel called.
I love my team.
I have a strong sense of responsibility.
I love meeting new challenges.
I am being rewarded financially.
I am creating a legacy.
I'm still enjoying what I do.

I want that for you too. I want you to find the joy of growth and apply that growth to your purpose. I want you to make a difference. And I want

> It's not what you are going to do, but it's what you are doing right now that counts.
>
> —NAPOLEON HILL

you to do it by developing the leader within you so that you can reach your potential, not only as a leader, but in every area of your life.

Paul Harvey said, "You can tell you're on the road to success because it is uphill all the way." The journey may be uphill, but as I explained in the previous chapter, everything worthwhile is uphill.

Growing into your leadership potential will take great time and effort. You will need to be highly intentional. You will have to work for it. You will have to spend your time and money to achieve it. Growth will not come to you. You must pursue it. Effective leadership doesn't happen on its own. You must go after it. But the journey is as important as the destination. Each step of your journey leads to new discoveries as well as the knowledge that there's more to learn.

Too many people want to know the end of the story before they are willing to take the first step. And that limits them. They've heard, "There is nothing new under the sun,"[8] so they stay home. They don't pursue growth. They wait for the discoveries of life to come to them, and they are always disappointed.

The real joy of the journey is that each step we take begins to unfold new discoveries. It is only after we've learned new things that we can look back and realize what we didn't know—and how much more there is to learn. And our new knowledge and discoveries become the motivation for us to continue the journey. Before long, we begin to realize that the destination isn't what we desire; rather, it is the growth we experience along the way. And we discover that there is no finish line.

Where will your growth journey take you? I don't know. I've gone farther and done much more than I ever dreamed of while growing up in the small town of Circleville, Ohio. Back then I couldn't have imagined where I am now.

So take the road that's open before you. Take a step. Make personal growth your daily habit. First, let the road take you where it leads. As you grow, begin to make choices at each juncture. Over time you will become more proactive, more directive, more intentional in where it leads you. But always remain open and teachable. Keep allowing yourself to be surprised every day. Grow into the person you have the potential to be. You'll never regret it.

DEVELOPING THE *LEARNER* WITHIN YOU

Because personal growth needs to be lifelong, what you do to grow in this area will be only the very beginning of a long but enjoyable journey. Start here, but revisit this process every six to twelve months.

ADOPT A LEARNER'S MIND-SET

Good leaders are learners. They are intentional. They want to learn from everyone they meet. They never arrive. They never feel that they know it all. And they are not afraid of having to unlearn some things and relearn others.

What is your mind-set about growth? What must you change in your attitude to become a better learner? Make the decision to learn something today and every day. Then tell others of your commitment so they can hold you accountable.

DEVELOP A SPECIFIC GROWTH STRATEGY

Growth is not automatic. You have to fight for it. And you have to make it a daily habit. Use the guidelines from the chapter to plan your growth strategy:

- **Big Picture: Where do I need to focus my growth?** If a growth plan is new for you, start with the basics. (What are they? Start with what *you* think they are. Ask a mentor or respected colleague what he or she thinks are the basics. That's your starting list.) If you're an old hand at personal growth, then focus on your strengths. Pick one to three areas where you want to grow. Then dig deep in one of those areas.
- **Measurement: How can I measure and affect my growth?** How will you know you're growing? How will you measure your progress? If you have a nebulous idea, something like, "I want to grow as a leader," you won't know whether you're improving. However,

223

if you instead decide to improve your communication skills as a leader and say, "In six months, I want to be able to do a polished, impacting, formal fifteen-minute presentation for work that will be praised by my colleagues, and I want to be able to speak clearly and decisively anytime I'm called upon in a meeting," then you have a measurable target to shoot for.

- **Consistency: *How can I grow daily?*** Personal growth needs to be a daily activity that develops into a daily habit. If you don't plan it, schedule it, and resource it, then it will never become that. Break down your measurable goal into growth steps you can take daily.
- **Application: *Can I act on it?*** As you review materials, target learning events, identify growth experiences, recruit mentors, and develop other strategies for your daily growth, always choose how you spend your time based on whether you can put what you're learning into practice.

I recommend that you reassess your growth targets regularly—quarterly, semiannually, or annually. During each assessment period, measure the progress you've made on your previous growth goals, and determine whether you need to create new ones. As I explained, I do this annually during the last week of December. I encourage you to find your own rhythm. And remember, this isn't a one-and-done activity. This is something you can do every year of your life.

What's Next?

When I wrote the original version of *Developing the Leader Within You* twenty-five years ago, I thought it was going to be my one leadership book. It hadn't occurred to me that I might have more to say about the subject. But I should have known better. Because I am continually working to grow and develop myself, how could I *not* have more to say on the subject? So I was grateful for the opportunity to update this book. And, of course, I've written other leadership books as well since 1993.

The process of developing the leader within you is a lifelong journey. If you have taken the time to read this book and you've done the assignments at the end of each chapter, I have no doubt that you have begun to see changes in your leadership ability. Your influence with others has grown. Your priorities are clearer and you act on them more decisively. You've won character battles. You've been able to initiate change and solve problems with greater ability. Your attitude is helping you to believe in people and serve them better. You have a vision for your leadership and more self-discipline to follow through with it. And you're learning more every day.

But this is only the beginning. The journey you have ahead of you can be an exciting one. I want to encourage you to keep expanding and growing your leadership skills. Keep working on the ten core areas I discuss in this book. Make use of the bonus materials at www.MaxwellLeader.com. Listen to podcasts. Read leadership books from other authors. I also want to recommend *The 21 Irrefutable Laws of Leadership* to you. It will give you specific leadership principles to live by.

I don't think it's possible for anyone to ever get to a place where he or she has learned everything there is to know about leadership. I'm seventy years old, I've spent almost fifty years studying leadership and practicing what I've learned, and I'm still growing. I feel that I'm like cellist Pablo Casals, who at eighty-one was asked why he still practiced for hours every day. His answer: "Because I think I am making progress."[1]

Adopt Casals's attitude and continue developing the leader within you. It will be one of the best things you ever do for yourself.

About the Author

John C. Maxwell is a #1 *New York Times* bestselling author, coach, and speaker who has sold more than 26 million books in fifty languages. In 2014 he was identified as the #1 leader in business by the American Management Association® and the most influential leadership expert in the world by *Business Insider* and *Inc.* magazines. He is the founder of the John Maxwell Company, the John Maxwell Team, EQUIP, and the John Maxwell Leadership Foundation, organizations that have trained millions of leaders. In 2015, they reached the milestone of having trained leaders from every country in the world. The recipient of the Mother Teresa Prize for Global Peace and Leadership from the Luminary Leadership Network, Dr. Maxwell speaks each year to *Fortune* 500 companies, presidents of nations, and many of the world's top business leaders. He can be followed at Twitter.com/JohnCMaxwell. For more information about him visit JohnMaxwell.com.

Notes

Chapter 1: The Definition of Leadership

1. James C. Georges, in an interview published in *Executive Communication*, January 1987.
2. J. R. Miller, *The Every Day of Life* (New York: Thomas Y. Crowell, 1892), 246–47.
3. Warren G. Bennis and Burt Nanus, *Leaders: Strategies for Taking Charge* (New York: Harper Business Essentials, 2003), 207.
4. Robert L. Dilenschneider, *Power and Influence: Mastering the Art of Persuasion* (New York: Prentice Hall, 1990), 8.
5. E. C. McKenzie, *Quips and Quotes* (Grand Rapids: Baker, 1980).
6. Fred Smith, *Learning to Lead: Bringing Out the Best in People* (Waco: Word, 1986), 117.
7. James Kouzes and Barry Posner, *The Leadership Challenge: How to Make Extraordinary Things Happen in Organizations*, 5th ed. (San Francisco: Jossey-Bass, 2012), 38.
8. "Influence," in Roy B. Zuck, ed., *The Speaker's Quote Book* (Grand Rapids: Kregel, 2009), 277.

Chapter 2: The Key to Leadership

1. Jamie Cornell, "Time Management: It's NOT About Time," *HuffPost's The Blog*, October 10, 2016, http://www.huffingtonpost.com/jamie-cornell/time-management-its-not-a_b_12407480.html?utm_hp_ref=business&ir=Business.
2. William James, *The Principles of Psychology* (New York: Henry and Holt, 1890), chap. 22.
3. Robert J. McKain, quoted in Tejgyan Global Foundation, *Great Thinkers Great Thoughts: One Thought Can Change Your World . . .* (N.p.: O! Publishing, 2012), chap. 44.

4. Dan S. Kennedy, "5 Time Management Techniques Worth Using," *Entrepreneur*, November 8, 2013, https://www.entrepreneur.com/article/229772.

5. Richard A. Swenson, *Margin: Restoring Emotional, Physical, Financial, and Time Reserves to Overloaded Lives* (Colorado Springs: NavPress, 2004), 69.

6. See John Maxwell, *The 21 Irrefutable Laws of Leadership*, 10th anniv. ed. (Nashville: Thomas Nelson, 2007), chap. 12.

7. "About Emotional Intelligence," TalentSmart, http://www.talentsmart.com /about/emotional-intelligence.php.

8. Tony Schwartz, "Relax! You'll Be More Productive," *New York Times*, February 9, 2013, http://www.nytimes.com/2013/02/10/opinion/sunday/relax -youll-be-more-productive.html.

9. Ibid.

Chapter 3: The Foundation of Leadership

1. Paul Vallely, *Pope Francis: Untying the Knots: The Struggle for the Soul of Catholicism*, rev. and exp. ed. (New York: Bloomsbury, 2015), 155.

2. Summarized from Gary Hamel, "The 15 Diseases of Leadership, According to Pope Francis," *Harvard Business Review*, April 14, 2015, https://hbr .org/2015/04/the-15-diseases-of-leadership-according-to-pope-francis.

3. Ibid.

4. David Kadalie, *Leader's Resource Kit: Tools and Techniques to Develop Your Leadership* (Nairobi: Evangel, 2006), 102.

5. Stephen M. R. Covey with Rebecca R. Merrill, *The Speed of Trust: One Thing That Changes Everything* (New York: Free Press, 2006), 14.

6. James M. Kouzes and Barry Z. Posner, "Without Trust You Cannot Lead," *Innovative Leader* 8, no. 2 (February 1999), http://www.winstonbrill.com /bril001/html/article_index/articles351_400.html.

7. Rob Brown, *Build Your Reputation: Grow Your Personal Brand for Career and Business Success* (West Sussex, UK: Wiley, 2016), 22–23.

8. Tim Irwin, *Derailed: Five Lessons Learned from Catastrophic Failures of Leadership* (Nashville: Thomas Nelson, 2009), 17.

9. Rosalina Chai, "Beauty of the Mosaic," Awakin.org, February 22, 2016, http://www.awakin.org/read/view.php?tid=2138.

10. David Gergen, "Character vs. Capacity," *U.S. News & World Report*, October 22, 2000.

11. Robert F. Morneau, *Humility: 31 Reflections on Christian Virtues* (Winona, MN: St. Mary's Press, 1997).

12. David Brooks, *The Road to Character* (New York: Random House, 2015), xii.
13. Ibid.
14. Parker J. Palmer, *A Hidden Wholeness: The Journey Toward an Undivided Life* (San Francisco: Wiley, 2004), 5.
15. Brooks, *Road to Character*, 14.
16. John Ortberg, *Soul Keeping* (Grand Rapids: Zondervan, 2014), 43.
17. Ibid., 46.
18. *Webster's New World Dictionary*, 3rd college ed., s.v. "integrity."
19. Ortberg, *Soul Keeping*, 103.
20. Tom Verducci, "The Rainmaker: How Cubs Boss Theo Epstein Ended a Second Epic Title Drought," *Sports Illustrated*, December 19, 2016, https://www.si.com/mlb/2016/12/14/theo-epstein-chicago-cubs-world-series-rainmaker.

CHAPTER 4: THE ULTIMATE TEST OF LEADERSHIP

1. Gordon S. White Jr., "Holtz Causes Orderly Success," *New York Times*, October 23, 1988, http://www.nytimes.com/1988/10/23/sports/college-football-holtz-causes-orderly-success.html.
2. Eric Harvey and Steve Ventura, *Forget for Success: Walking Away from Outdated, Counterproductive Beliefs and People Practices* (Dallas: Performance, 1997), 12.
3. Ibid., 2–3.
4. Malcolm Gladwell, "The Big Man Can't Shoot" (podcast), Revisionist History, episode 3, http://revisionisthistory.com/episodes/03-the-big-man-cant-shoot, accessed February 10, 2017.
5. "Wilt Chamberlain," Basketball Reference, http://www.basketball-reference.com/players/c/chambwi01.html, accessed February 10, 2017.
6. "Rick Barry," Basketball Reference, http://www.basketball-reference.com/players/b/barryri01.html, accessed February 10, 2017.
7. "Transcript: Choosing Wrong," This American Life from WBEZ (website), June 24, 2016, https://www.thisamericanlife.org/radio-archives/episode/590/transcript, accessed February 10, 2017.
8. Gladwell, "The Big Man Can't Shoot."
9. Adapted from Lightbulbjokes.com, http://www.lightbulbjokes.com/directory/a.html, accessed February 8, 2017.
10. Rick Warren, "Why Your Way Isn't Working," Crosswalk.com, July 12, 2016, http://www.crosswalk.com/devotionals/daily-hope-with-rick-warren/daily-hope-with-rick-warren-july-12-2016.html.

11. "Madmen They Were. The Greatest Pitch of Them All. True Story," *StreamAbout* (blog), March 23, 2012, http://streamabout.blogspot.com /2012/03/madmen-they-were-greatest-pitch-of-them.html.

12. "Peter Marsh, Advertising Executive—Obituary," *Telegraph*, April 12, 2016, http://www.telegraph.co.uk/obituaries/2016/04/12/peter-marsh -advertising-executive-obituary/.

13. Samuel R. Chand, *8 Steps to Achieve Your Destiny: Lead Your Life with Purpose* (New Kensington, PA: Whitaker House, 2016), Kindle edition, loc. 997 of 1895.

14. Mac Anderson, *212 Leadership: The 10 Rules for Highly Effective Leadership* (Napierville, IL: Simple Truths, 2011), Kindle edition, 33–34.

15. Paraphrase of a statement made by Robert Kennedy in May 1964 during a speech at the University of Pennsylvania.

16. Mac Anderson and Tom Feltenstein, *Change Is Good . . . You Go First: 21 Ways to Inspire Change* (Napierville, IL: Sourcebooks, 2015). Italics are in the original.

17. Winston Churchill, *His Complete Speeches, 1897–1963*, ed. Robert Rhodes James, vol. 4 (1922–1928) (N.p.: Chelsea House, 1974), 3706.

18. Maxwell, *The 21 Irrefutable Laws of Leadership*, 169.

CHAPTER 5: THE QUICKEST WAY TO GAIN LEADERSHIP

1. M. Scott Peck, *The Road Less Traveled* (New York: Touchstone, 1978), 15.

2. See Paul Larkin, "3 Principles of Pragmatic Leaders," LinkedIn, July 19, 2015, https://www.linkedin.com/pulse/3-principles-pragmatic-leaders -paul-larkin/.

3. Jim Collins, *Good to Great*, (New York: Harper Collins, 2001), 81.

4. "Expectancy-Value Theory of Motivation, Psychology Concepts, http:// www.psychologyconcepts.com/expectancy-value-theory-of-motivation/, accessed February 14, 2017.

5. Louis E. Bisch, "Spiritual Insight," *Leaves of Grass*, Clyde Francis Lytle, ed. (Fort Worth: Brownlow, 1948), 14.

6. Maxwell, *The 21 Irrefutable Laws of Leadership*, 103.

7. Victor Goertzel and Mildred Goertzel, *Cradles of Eminence*, 2nd ed. (Boston: Great Potential Press, 1978), 282.

8. Glenn Llopis, "The 4 Most Effective Ways Leaders Solve Problems," *Forbes*, November 4, 2013, http://www.forbes.com/sites/glennllopis/2013 /11/04/the-4-most-effective-ways-leaders-solve-problems/#397e9edf2bda.

9. Max De Pree, *Leadership Is an Art* (N.p.: Crown Business, 2004), 11.

10. Adapted from a joke by Henny Youngman included in Warren Buffett's Berkshire Hathaway, Inc., 1991 Letter to Shareholders, http://www.berkshire hathaway.com/letters/1991.html, accessed February 9, 2017.

11. Llopis, "The 4 Most Effective Ways Leaders Solve Problems."

12. Larkin, "3 Principles of Pragmatic Leaders."

13. "John F. Kennedy and PT 109," John F. Kennedy Presidential Library and Museum, https://www.jfklibrary.org/JFK/JFK-in-History/John-F-Kennedy -and-PT109.aspx, accessed February 9, 2017.

Chapter 6: The Extra Plus in Leadership

1. "Charles R. Swindoll: Quotes: Quotable Quote," Goodreads, http://www .goodreads.com/quotes/267482-the-longer-i-live-the-more-i-realize-the -impact, accessed September 25, 2017.

2. Robert E. Quinn, *Deep Change: Discovering the Leader Within* (San Francisco: Jossey-Bass, 1996), 21.

3. Nell Mohney, "Beliefs Can Influence Attitudes," *Kingsport Times-News*, July 25, 1986, 48.

4. Danny Cox with John Hoover, *Leadership When the Heat's On*, 2nd ed. (New York: McGraw-Hill, 2002), 88.

5. "Elisha Gray and the Telephone," ShoreTel website, https://www.shoretel .com/elisha-gray-and-telephone, accessed March 1, 2017.

6. Adapted from his article "Success Principles: Do You Feel Lucky—or Fortunate?" SuccessNet.org, http://successnet.org/cms/success-principles17 /lucky-fortunate, accessed June 5, 2017.

7. Richard Jerome, "Charlton Heston 1923–2008," *People* magazine, April 21, 2008, http://people.com/archive/charlton-heston-1923-2008-vol-69-no-15/.

8. Tim Hansel, *Through the Wilderness of Loneliness* (Chicago: D. C. Cook, 1991), 128.

9. T. Boone Pickens, in *The Ultimate Handbook of Motivational Quotes for Coaches and Leaders*, ed. Pat Williams with Ken Hussar (Monterey, CA: Coaches Choice, 2011), chap. 2.

10. Diane Coutu, "Creativity Step by Step," *Harvard Business Review*, April 2008, https://hbr.org/2008/04/creativity-step-by-step.

11. Allison Eck, "Don't Just Finish Your Project, Evolve It," 99U, http://99u.com /articles/52033/do-you-have-a-jazz-mindset-or-a-classical-mindset, accessed September 25, 2017.

12. Ibid.
13. Sarah Rapp, "Why Success Always Starts with Failure," 99U, http://99u .com/articles/7072/why-success-always-starts-with-failure, accessed February 21, 2017.
14. Heidi Grant Halvorson, "Why You Should Give Yourself Permission to Screw Up," 99U, http://99u.com/articles/7273/why-you-should-give -yourself-permission-to-screw-up, accessed March 6, 2017.
15. Kouzes and Posner, *The Leadership Challenge.*
16. Mark Batterson, *Chase the Lion: If Your Dream Doesn't Scare You, It's Too Small* (New York: Multnomah, 2016), ix.

Chapter 7: The Heart of Leadership

1. Ephesians 4:11–12 NIV.
2. "The Servant as Leader," Robert K. Greenleaf Center for Servant Leadership, https://www.greenleaf.org/what-is-servant-leadership/, accessed March 9, 2017.
3. Eugene B. Habecker, *The Other Side of Leadership* (Wheaton, IL: Victor Books, 1987), 217.
4. 1 Timothy 6:17–19 MSG.
5. S. Chris Edmonds, *The Culture Engine: A Framework for Driving Results, Inspiring Your Employees, and Transforming Your Workplace* (Hoboken: John Wiley and Sons, 2014), 67.
6. Ann McGee-Cooper and Duane Trammell, "From Hero-as-Leader to Servant-as-Leader," *Focus on Leadership: Servant-Leadership for the Twenty-First Century*, ed. Larry C. Spears and Michele Lawrence (New York: John Wiley and Sons, 2002), Kindle edition, loc. 1623 of 4168.
7. "Pope to Deacons: 'You Are Called to Serve, Not Be Self-Serving,'" Vatican Radio, May 29, 2016, http://en.radiovaticana.va/news/2016/05/29 /pope_to_deacons_'you_are_called_to_serve,_not_to_be_self-se/1233321.
8. Song used with permission.
9. Dan Price, "Become a Servant Leader in 4 Steps," *Success*, January 25, 2017, http://www.success.com/article/become-a-servant-leader-in-4-steps.
10. Alan Loy McGinnis, *Bringing Out the Best in People: How to Enjoy Helping Others Excel* (Minneapolis: Augsburg Books, 1985), 177.
11. Jim Heskett, "Why Isn't 'Servant Leadership' More Prevalent?" Working Knowledge (Harvard Business School), May 1, 2013, http://hbswk.hbs.edu /item/why-isnt-servant-leadership-more-prevalent.

CHAPTER 8: THE INDISPENSABLE QUALITY OF LEADERSHIP

1. Andy Stanley, *Visioneering: God's Blueprint for Developing and Maintaining Vision* (Colorado Springs: Multnomah, 1999), 9.
2. James Allen, *As a Man Thinketh* (N.p.: Shandon Press, 2017), Kindle edition, loc. 329 of 394.
3. Ibid., loc. 75 of 394.
4. William P. Barker, *A Savior for All Seasons* (Old Tappan, NJ: Fleming H. Revell, 1986), 175–76.
5. Luis Palau, *Dream Great Dreams* (Colorado Springs: Multnomah, 1984).
6. Kenneth Hildebrand, *Achieving Real Happiness* (New York: Harper & Brothers, 1955).
7. Rick Warren, "The Crucial Difference Between Managing and Leading," Pastors.com, July 31, 2015, http://pastors.com/the-crucial-difference -between-managing-and-leading/.
8. Napoleon Hill, as quoted in Barry Farber, *Diamond Power: Gems of Wisdom from America's Greatest Marketer* (Franklin Lakes, NJ: Career Press, 2003), 53.
9. As quoted in Michael Nason and Donna Nason, *Robert Schuller: The Inside Story* (Waco: Word Books, 1983).
10. Judith B. Meyerowitz, "The Vocational Fantasies of Men and Women at Mid-life" (doctoral dissertation, Columbia University, 1989).
11. See John Maxwell, *The 15 Invaluable Laws of Growth* (New York: Center Street, 2012), chap. 7.
12. As quoted in Dianna Daniels Booher, *Executive's Portfolio of Model Speeches for All Occasions* (New York: Prentice Hall, 1991), 34.
13. John Maxwell, *Good Leaders Ask Great Questions* (New York: Center Street, 2014), 6.
14. See chapter 1 in John Maxwell, *Put Your Dreams to the Test* (Nashville: Thomas Nelson, 2011).
15. See Maxwell, *The 21 Irrefutable Laws*, chap. 19.
16. "Andy Stanley—Chick-Fil-A Leadercast 2013," The Sermon Notes, May 10, 2013, http://www.thesermonnotes.com/andy-stanley-chick-fil-a -leadercast-2013/.
17. Donald T. Phillips, *Martin Luther King, Jr. on Leadership: Inspiration and Wisdom for Challenging Times* (New York: Warner Books, 1998), 97.
18. George S. Patton, "Mechanized Forces: A Lecture," *Cavalry Journal* (September–October 1933), in J. Furman Daniel III, ed., *21st Century*

Patton: Strategic Insights for the Modern Era (Annapolis, MD: Naval Institute Press, 2016), 142.

19. Tim Worstall, "Steve Jobs and the Don't Settle Speech," *Forbes*, October 8, 2011, https://www.forbes.com/sites/timworstall/2011/10/08 /steve-jobs-and-the-dont-settle-speech/#4a2544f87437.

Chapter 9: The Price Tag of Leadership

1. "Temperance (1466) egkráteia," SermonIndex.net (Greek Word Studies), accessed April 17, 2017, http://www.sermonindex.net/modules/articles /index.php?view=article&aid=35940.
2. Edgar A. Guest, "Keep Going," *Brooklyn Daily Eagle*, February 24, 1953, 8, https://www.newspapers.com/clip/1709402/keep_going_poem_by_edgar _a_guest/.
3. Brian Tracy, *The Power of Discipline: 7 Ways It Can Change Your Life* (Naperville, IL: Simple Truths, 2008), 6–7.
4. Rory Vaden, *Take the Stairs: 7 Steps to Achieving True Success* (New York: Perigee, 2012), 35–36.
5. Ibid., 38.
6. Attributed to Dennis P. Kimbro in Jeorald Pitts and Lil Tone, "Can You Identify What I Am?" *Los Angeles Sentinel*, December 16, 2010, http:// www.lasentinel.net/can-you-identify-what-i-am.html.
7. Proverbs 23:7.
8. Gary Keller with Jay Papasan, *The ONE Thing: The Surprisingly Simple Truth Behind Extraordinary* (N.p.: Bard Press, 2013).
9. "Biography," LouisLamour.com, http://www.louislamour.com/aboutlouis /biography6.htm, accessed April 20, 2017.
10. "3,000 Hits Club," MLB.com, http://mlb.mlb.com/mlb/history/milestones /index.jsp?feature=three_thousand_h, accessed April 19, 2017.

Chapter 10: The Expansion of Leadership

1. Maxwell, *The 15 Invaluable Laws of Growth*, 156.
2. Eric Hoffer, *Reflections on the Human Condition* (New York: Harper & Row, 1973), 22.
3. Gail Sheehy, *Passages: Predictable Crises of Adult Life* (New York: Ballantine, 2006), 499.
4. Quoted in Alvin Toffler, *Future Shock* (New York: Bantam Books, 1970), 414.

5. David D. Lewis Jr. Personal Development Page, Facebook, November 12, 2014, https://www.facebook.com/DreamUnstuck/posts/743099232444718.

6. Maxwell, *The 15 Invaluable Laws of Growth*, 5.

7. Dolly Parton, Twitter, April 8, 2015, https://twitter.com/dollyparton/status/585890099583397888?lang=en.

8. Ecclesiastes 1:9.

What's Next?

1. Quoted in Leonard Lyons, Lyons Den, *Daily Defender* (Chicago), November 4, 1958, page 5, col. 1.

transforming
LEADERS
transforming
COUNTRIES

Together,
WE CAN CHANGE THE WORLD.
jmlf.org

SUCCESS OR SIGNIFICANCE?
WHAT'S YOUR STORY?

MOBILIZING LEADERS FOR
TRANSFORMATION

iequip.church | 678.225.3300